Living in Elizabethan England

Titles in the Series Include:

Living in Elizabethan England

Myra Weatherly, *Book Editor*

Bruce Glassman, *Vice President*
Bonnie Szumski, *Publisher*
Helen Cothran, *Managing Editor*

GREENHAVEN
PRESS ®

San Diego • Detroit • New York • San Francisco • Cleveland
New Haven, Conn. • Waterville, Maine • London • Munich

LIBRARY OF CONGRESS CATALOGING-IN-PUBLICATION DATA

Living in Elizabethan England / Myra Weatherly, book editor.
  p. cm. — (Exploring cultural history)
Includes bibliographical references and index.
ISBN 0-7377-2088-3 (lib. : alk. paper)
  1. England—Social life and customs—16th century. 2. Great Britain—History—Elizabeth, 1558–1603. I. Weatherly, Myra. II. Series.
DA320.L57 2004
942.05'5—dc22
                                                                    2003056834

Printed in the United States of America

Contents

Chapter 1: The Living Environment

1. Houses and Their Furnishings
   by William Harrison   16
   The dwellings of Elizabethans were the focus of all aspects of life. They were born in their homes, died in
   their homes, and many worked out of their homes. The
   nature of one's house varied according to social class as
   well as location.

2. Family Lifestyles
   by Norah Lofts   21
   In Elizabethan England the standard of living increased
   for all except the lowest classes. In addition to housing,
   the rise of prosperity and stability had an impact on
   food and dress.

3. The Role of Servants
   by Lu Emily Pearson   28
   For Elizabethans the household was the basic social
   unit, in which the head exercised a responsibility similar to the monarch. They believed that discipline, order,
   and godliness in the household, which included servants as well as family members, formed the basis for a
   healthy state.

4. Elizabethan Travel at Home
   by M. St. Clare Byrne   35
   In Elizabethan times throngs of robbers, vagabonds,
   and beggars terrorized travelers, including the queen,
   on the open road and constituted one of the most
   pressing social problems of the day.

Chapter 2: In Society: Politics, Religion, Marriage and Family, Education

Chapter 3: Arts, Entertainment, and Leisure Pursuits

Foreword

Too often, history books and teachers place an overemphasis on events and dates. Students learn that key births, battles, revolutions, coronations, and assassinations occurred in certain years. But when many centuries separate these happenings from the modern world, they can seem distant, disconnected, even irrelevant.

The reality is that today's society is *not* disconnected from the societies that preceded it. In fact, modern culture is a sort of melting pot of various aspects of life in past cultures. Over the course of centuries and millennia, one culture passed on some of its traditions, in the form of customs, habits, ideas, and beliefs, to another, which modified and built on them to fit its own needs. That culture then passed on its own version of the traditions to later cultures, including today's. Pieces of everyday life in past cultures survive in our own lives, therefore. And it is often these morsels of tradition, these survivals of tried and true past experience, that people most cherish, take comfort in, and look to for guidance. As the great English scholar and archaeologist Sir Leonard Woolley put it, "We cannot divorce ourselves from our past. We are always conscious of precedents . . . and we let experience shape our views and actions."

Thus, for example, Americans and the inhabitants of a number of other modern nations can pride themselves on living by the rule of law, educating their children in formal schools, expressing themselves in literature and art, and following the moral precepts of various religions and philosophies. Yet modern society did not invent the laws, schools, literature, art, religions, and philosophies that pervade it; rather, it inherited these things from previous cultures. "Time, the great destroyer, is also the great preserver," the late, noted thinker Herbert J. Muller once observed. "It has preserved . . . the immense accumulation of products, skills, styles, customs, institutions, and ideas that make the man on the American street indebted to all the peoples of history, including some who never saw a street." In this way, ancient Mesopotamia gave the world its first cities and literature; ancient Egypt, large-scale architecture; ancient Israel, the formative concepts of Judaism,

Christianity, and Islam; ancient Greece, democracy, the theater, Olympic sports, and magnificent ceramics; ancient China, gunpowder and exotic fabrics; ancient Rome and medieval England, their pioneering legal systems; Renaissance Italy, great painting and sculpture; Elizabethan England, the birth of modern drama; and colonial America, the formative environments of the founders of the United States, the most powerful and prosperous nation in world history. Only by looking back on those peoples and how they lived can modern society understand its roots.

Not all the products of cultural history have been so constructive, however. Most ancient Greeks severely restricted the civil rights and daily lives of women, for instance; the Romans kept and abused large numbers of slaves, as did many Americans in the years preceding the Civil War; and Nazi Germany and the Soviet Union curbed or suppressed freedom of speech, assembly, and religion. Examining these negative aspects of life in various past cultures helps to expose the origins of many of the social problems that exist today; it also reminds us of the ever-present potential for people to make mistakes and pursue misguided or destructive social and economic policies.

The books in the Greenhaven Press Exploring Cultural History series provide readers with the major highlights of life in human cultures from ancient times to the present. The family, home life, food and drink, women's duties and rights, childhood and education, arts and leisure, literacy and literature, roads and means of communications, slavery, religious beliefs, and more are examined in essays grouped by theme. The essays in each volume have been chosen for their readability and edited to manageable lengths. Many are primary sources. These original voices from a past culture echo through the corridors of time and give the volume a strong feeling of immediacy and authenticity. The other essays are by historians and other modern scholars who specialize in the culture in question. An annotated table of contents, chronology, and extensive bibliography broken down by theme add clarity and context. Thus, each volume in the Greenhaven Press Exploring Cultural History series opens a unique window through which readers can gaze into a distant time and place and eavesdrop on life in a long vanished culture.

Introduction:
Queen Elizabeth's Torch

Queen Elizabeth could be called the first feminist or the first spinmaster. Not only was Elizabeth a ruler by character as well as vocation, she was also a supreme actress. She knew precisely when to use her charm. This larger-than-life royal made England a mighty nation and inspired a flowering of enduring literature, drama, music, and poetry.

Remembering Elizabeth

Elizabeth remains a figure of great interest today. Four centuries after her death, her portraits—red hair studded with pearls, a lace ruff, and ghostly white face—are as recognizable as a movie star's. In 2003 a number of new exhibitions and tributes designed to commemorate the four-hundred-year anniversary of the Virgin Queen's death opened in London and North America. Several new biographies commemorate her reign, adding to Elizabeth's distinction of being the most written about woman in history. The results of a recent BBC television poll of Britons showed Elizabeth I to be the best known and most admired English monarch.

The Mystique of Elizabeth I

What inspired such great and long-lasting devotion among her subjects and throughout history has baffled many highly regarded historians. Modern author Jasper Ridley shares this confusion:

> The prestige of kingship does not entirely explain the devotion which she inspired among her contemporaries. There must have been some other reason why the MPs in the House of Commons, who clashed with her in nearly every Parliament, were devoted to her; why [John] Harrington, after telling one discreditable story after another about her, repeatedly expressed his admiration for her; why John Stubbs called out "God save the Queen!" when his hand was cut off at her orders and why most of her subjects, and most historians for four hundred years, have given her the credit for every success and have been prepared to overlook all her faults. There must have been something which won them over but which we cannot easily grasp today—her charm, her courage,

her charisma, and her magic—which fascinated her subjects and descendants for twelve generations.[1]

British author M. St. Clare Byrne, noted twentieth-century writer of the social history of the Elizabethan Age, describes the relationship between Elizabeth and her subjects based on primary documents. Byrne writes:

Queen Elizabeth commanded the loyalty and admiration of her subjects throughout her reign. She remained a beloved figure long after her death.

It is no mere literalism to say that without Elizabeth there would have been no Elizabethan Age. The Tudors all had powerful and interesting personalities, but it is significant that only the last one has given her name to an epoch. . . . Her character was the right one for the situation—it made her alive to the needs of the moment, and it made her sensitive to the feeling of the nation as none of her predecessors had ever been. . . . Hence she became to them almost the incarnation of their nationalism, as well as its focus and its directive genius.[2]

One quality of Elizabeth's that seems to have made her a remarkable leader was her oratory talent. According to professor of English Leah S. Marcus,

As we begin a new century, her work is of increasing interest to historians and literary scholars. Her reputation as a writer is arguably higher now than it has been at any time since her own era. . . . Elizabeth usually gets high marks for her diplomatic skills, but we have not fully acknowledged how much of her success can be traced to her brilliance with language.[3]

In her famous Armada speech, which she delivered astride a gray horse and wearing a silver breastplate, she addressed her troops at Tilbury prior to the Spanish invasion:

I am come amongst you as you see, at this time, not for my recreation and disport, but being resolved in the midst and heat of battle, to live or die amongst you all, and to lay down for my God and for my kingdom. . . . For I know I have a body of a weak and feeble woman, but I have the heart and stomach of a King, and a King of England, too.[4]

Her words stirred national pride and confidence in her countrymen. They also served as a warning to any European nation that dared to invade England. The defeat of the Armada signaled the beginning of England's reign as a sea power and eventually led to the creation of the British Empire.

By the end of Elizabeth's reign, her oratorical powers had become legendary. Her last and greatest public utterance was delivered before Parliament on November 30, 1601. She reflected on her long reign. For those who heard it and for generations to come, Elizabeth's Golden Speech lived on in their memories. She declared: "Though you have had many and may have many more mighty and wise sitting in this seat, yet you never had or shall have any that will be more careful and loving."[5]

A Living Age

Some of Queen Elizabeth's most formative influences on her people live on today. In his book, *The England of Elizabeth*, Elizabethan scholar A.L. Rowse contends:

> The Elizabethan Age is not something dead and apart from us; it is alive and all round us and within us. Wherever one goes in England there are visible memorials of what those men and women were when they were alive, the houses they built and loved and lived in, the things they made and wore, the objects they cherished, the patterns they imposed upon the very landscape; wherever English people are gathered together, or—and here is the miracle—wherever they speak the language, something of the tradition goes on in them.[6]

Not only the English but people everywhere—who at one time or another were part of the great British Empire—owe much of their culture to Elizabeth's England. Shortly after her death it became clear that the reign of Elizabeth would not be forgotten. Historian William Camden wrote in the seventeenth century: "No oblivion shall ever bury the Glory of her Name for her happy and reknowned Memory still liveth, and shall for ever live in the Minds of men to all Posterity, as of one who . . . In Wisdome and Felicity of Government surpassed . . . all the Princes since the days of Augustus."[7]

Notes

1. Jasper Ridley, *Elizabeth I: The Shrewdness of Virtue.* New York: Viking, 1988, p. 338.
2. M. St. Clare Byrne, *Elizabethan Life in Town and Country.* London: Methune, 1961, p. 16.
3. Leah S. Marcus, "Elizabeth the Writer," *History Today*, October 2000, p. 36.
4. Quoted in Lacey Baldwin Smith, *The Horizon Book of the Elizabethan World.* New York: American Heritage, 1967, p. 289.
5. Quoted in Doug Stewart, "Reign On," *Smithsonian*, June 2003, p. 64.
6. A.L. Rowse, *The England of Elizabeth.* New York: Macmillan, 1950, p. 23.
7. Quoted in Susan Watkins, *The Public and Private Worlds of Elizabeth I.* New York: Thames and Hudson, 1998, p. 197.

The Living Environment

CHAPTER
1

Chapter Preface

For most Elizabethans, life activities centered around the home, more so than today. People were born in their homes. They died in their homes. Many worked out of their homes. The average person never traveled more than half a day's walk from home.

Most Elizabethans lived and worked in small communities. All the necessities of life were homegrown or homemade. It was a life ordered by sunrise and sunset as well as by the cycles of planting and harvesting. The average person's needs could be met without ever leaving home or traveling on dangerous roads.

The village was the center of social life. Everyone knew everyone else. The break in their routine occurred on Sundays when the villagers met for church in the morning. They spent the afternoon gossiping and having a few pints of ale. While the women spent their time sewing or spinning, the men and children played games.

In a world of little mobility, families remained close in proximity and in spirit. Everyone belonged to a clan of brothers, sisters, parents, grandparents, aunts, uncles, cousins, and kin by marriage.

In contrast to the life of common people, life in Elizabethan England for the nobility was lavish and sophisticated. School-master Henry Peacham wrote of the nobility: "Noblemen or gentlemen ought to be preferred in fees, honours, offices and other dignities of command and government before the common people."

To maintain their image and status, the nobles of the Elizabethan era kept up huge households and dressed opulently. They engaged in a variety of social activities including grand masques and balls. Many rich families had homes in London as well as in the country. They traveled and even made sea voyages. When the nobility died, they were buried in style. Elaborate monuments of marble or stone mark their resting places.

By modern day standards, life in the second half of the sixteenth century was rough. Disease, suffering, poverty, and poor nutrition plagued many people. Yet in many ways, Elizabethans had the same problems and concerns as modern people do today.

Houses and Their Furnishings

William Harrison

Originally written in 1587 as part of Raphael Holinshed's historical chronicles of England, Scotland, and Wales, *The Description of England* by William Harrison ranks as a classic of social description. Harrison, country rector and historian, recorded facts about the changing England in which he lived. He gathered these facts from books, letters, maps, conversations, and his own observations and experiences. His compilations provide a richly detailed study of nearly every aspect of Elizabethan life: food and diet, palaces and houses, laws, clothing, dogs, cattle, punishments for criminals, natural resources, armaments and the navy, thoroughfares, rivers, and much more.

In the following essay taken from *The Description of England*, Harrison points out that English houses varied with the availability of building materials in the various parts of the country. The author also notes the effects of the growing prosperity of the country in respect to houses and their furnishings.

The greatest part of our building in the cities and good towns of England consisteth only of timber, for as yet few of the houses of the commonalty (except here and there in the West Country towns) are made of stone, although they may (in my opinion) in divers other places be builded so good cheap of the one as of the other. In old time the houses of the Britons were slightly set up with a few posts and many raddles [interwoven supple sticks], with stable and all offices under one roof, the like whereof almost is to be seen in the fenny countries and northern parts unto this day, where for lack of wood they are enforced to continue this ancient manner of building. It is not in vain, therefore, in speaking of building, to make a distinction between the plain and woody soils; for as in these our houses are com-

William Harrison, *The Description of England: The Classic Contemporary Account of Tudor Social Life*, edited by Georges Edelen. New York: Dover Publications, Inc., 1994.

monly strong and well-timbered—so that in many places there are not above four, six, or nine inches between stud and stud—so in the open and champaign countries they are enforced for want of stuff to use no studs at all but only frank posts, rasens, beams, prick posts, groundsels, summers (or dormants), transoms, and such principals, with here and there a girding [supporting beam], whereunto they fasten their splints or raddles, and then cast it all over with thick clay to keep out the wind, which otherwise would annoy them. . . .

In like sort, as every country house is thus appareled on the outside, so is it inwardly divided into sundry rooms above and beneath; and where plenty of wood is, they cover them with tiles [shingles], otherwise with straw, sedge, or reed, except some quarry of slate be near-hand, from whence they have for their money so much as may suffice them. . . .

Inside Houses

In plastering likewise of our fairest houses over our heads, we use to lay first a lain [layer] or two of white mortar tempered with hair upon laths, which are nailed one by another (or sometimes upon reed or wickers, more dangerous for fire, and made fast here and there with sap-laths, for falling down), and finally cover all with the aforesaid plaster, which beside the delectable whiteness of the stuff itself is laid on so even and smoothly as nothing in my judgment can be done with more exactness. The walls of our houses on the inner sides in like sort be either hanged with tapestry, arras work, or painted cloths, wherein either divers histories, or herbs, beasts, knots, and suchlike are stained, or else they are ceiled [paneled] with oak of our own or wainscot brought hither out of the East [Baltic] countries, whereby the rooms are not a little commended, made warm, and much more close than otherwise they would be. As for stoves, we have not hitherto used them greatly, yet do they now begin to be made in divers houses of the gentry and wealthy citizens, who build them not to work and feed in, as in Germany and elsewhere, but now and then to sweat in, as occasion and need shall require it. . . .

Of old time our country houses instead of glass did use much lattice, and that made either of wicker or fine rifts [strips] of oak in checkerwise. . . .

But now these are not in use, so that only the clearest glass is most esteemed; for we have diverse sorts, some brought out of Burgundy, some out of Normandy, much out of Flanders, beside that which is made in England, which would be so good as the best if we were diligent and careful to bestow more cost upon it, and yet as it is each one that may will have it for his building.

Houses of Gentlemen

Moreover the mansion houses [dwellings] of our country towns and villages (which in champaign ground stand all together by streets and joining one to another but in woodland soils dispersed here and there, each one upon the several grounds of their owners) are builded in such sort generally as that they have neither dairy, stable, nor brewhouse annexed unto them under the same roof (as in many places beyond the sea and some of the north parts of our country) but all separate from the first and one of them from another. And yet for all this they are not so far distant in sunder but that the goodman lying in his bed may lightly hear what is done in each of them with ease and call quickly unto his meinie [household] if any danger should attach [seize] him.

The ancient manors and houses of our gentlemen are yet, and for the most part, of strong timber, in framing whereof our carpenters have been and are worthily preferred before those of like science among all other nations. Howbeit, such as be lately builded are commonly either of brick or hard stone or both, their rooms large and comely, and houses of office further distant from their lodgings. Those of the nobility are likewise wrought with brick and hard stone, as provision may best be made, but so magnificent and stately as the basest house of a baron doth often match in our days with some honors of princes in old time. . . .

The furniture of our houses also exceedeth and is grown in manner even to passing delicacy; and herein I do not speak of the nobility and gentry only but likewise of the lowest sort in most places of our South Country that have anything at all to take to. Certes in noblemen's houses it is not rare to see abundance of arras, rich hangings of tapestry, silver vessel, and so much other plate as may furnish sundry cupboards, to the sum oftentimes of £1,000 or £2,000 at the least, whereby the value of this and the rest of their stuff doth grow to be almost inestimable. Likewise in the houses of knights, gentlemen, merchantmen, and some other wealthy citizens, it is not geason [uncommon] to behold generally their great provision of tapestry, Turkey work [tapestry from Turkey], pewter, brass, fine linen, and thereto costly cupboards of plate, worth £500 or £600 or £1,000, to be deemed by estimation. But as herein all these sorts do far exceed their elders and predecessors, and in neatness and curiosity the merchant all other, so in time past the costly furniture stayed there, whereas now it is descended yet lower, even unto the inferior artificers and many farmers, who, by virtue of their old and not of their new leases, have for the most part learned also to garnish their cupboards with plate, their joint beds with tapestry and silk hangings, and their tables with carpets and fine napery, whereby the wealth of our country (God be praised therefor and give us grace to employ it well) doth infinitely appear. . . .

There are old men yet dwelling in the village where I remain which have noted three things to be marvelously altered in England within their sound remembrance, and other three things too-too much increased. One is the multitude of chimneys lately erected, whereas in their young days there were not above two or three, if so many, in most uplandish towns of the realm (the religious houses and manor places of their lords always excepted, and peradventure some great personages), but each one made his fire against a reredos [back of an open hearth] in the hall, where he dined and dressed his meat.

The second is the great (although not general) amendment of lodging, for (said they) our fathers, yea, and we ourselves also, have lien [lain] full oft upon straw pallets, on rough mats covered only with a sheet, under coverlets made of dagswain or hapharlots [rough materials] (I use their own terms), and a good round log under their heads instead of a bolster or pillow. If it were so that our fathers or the goodman of the house had within seven years after his marriage purchased a mattress or flock-bed, and thereto a sack of chaff to rest his head upon, he thought himself to be as well lodged as the lord of the town, that peradventure lay seldom in a bed of down or whole feathers, so well were they contented and with such base kind of furniture, which also is not very much amended as yet in some parts of Bedfordshire and elsewhere further off from our southern parts. Pillows (said they) were thought meet only for women in childbed. As for servants, if they had any sheet above them it was well, for seldom had they any under their bodies to keep them from the pricking straws that ran oft through the canvas of the pallet and rased their hardened hides.

The third thing they tell of is the exchange of vessel, as of treen [wooden] platters into pewter, and wooden spoons into silver or tin. For so common were all sorts of treen stuff in old time that a man should hardly find four pieces of pewter (of which one was peradventure a salt) in a good farmer's house, and yet for all this frugality (if it may so be justly called) they were scarce able to live and pay their rents at their days without selling of a cow or an horse or more.

Family Lifestyles

Norah Lofts

Popular English writer Norah Lofts grew up on a farm near Shipdham, Norfolk. As a child she wrote stories. In adulthood, she became a prolific writer, producing as many as eighty books in her lifetime. Her works include biographies and nonfiction as well as novels depicting historical figures and re-creations of historical crimes. In the following selection, excerpted from her nonfiction work, *Domestic Life in England*, Lofts points out that many Elizabethan households included extended family members. She also examines the style of family life in Elizabethan times from the richest to the poorest in a way that brings history alive.

B ehind the gracious facade of the Tudor houses a more domesticated style of family life was developing, partly due to the peace and stability of the age, and partly to the civilizing influence of Renaissance ideas and to the growing popularity of domestic amusements such as reading, conversation, gardening and musicmaking. Erasmus has left a pleasant picture of the family of Sir Thomas More in the reign of Henry VIII. He wrote to a friend: 'More hath builte near London upon the Thames side, a commodius house, neither meane nor subject to envie, yet magnificent enough; there he converseth affably with his family, his wife, his son and daughter-in-lawe, his three daughters and their husbands, with eleven grandchildren.'

It was common for a house to contain more than the immediate family: it was a haven for any relation who through widowhood, or failure to marry, or loss of parents, was in need of a home.

Children were still strictly brought up but the relationship with their parents seems to have become more affectionate. Even Elizabeth's stern secretary, William Cecil, could write a charming poem to his daughter Ann accompanying the gift of a spinning wheel.

But one thing first I wish and pray,
Lest thirst of thrift might soon you tire
Only to spin one pound a day
And play the rest as time require.

His affection was not strong enough to turn him from the advantages of marrying her to a young wastrel, the Earl of Oxford, but he did welcome Ann and her children back to his roof when the marriage broke up. When Cecil was an old man it was said of him: 'If he could get his table set round with young children he was then in his kingdom. He was happy in most worldly things, but most happy in his children and children's children.'

Boys were still sent away from home, but more often to school and university to be educated in the arts and sciences than to a noble household to learn the art of war, as had been the medieval custom. The gentry were not ashamed to apprentice their younger sons to trade and this helped to avert the deep division between the classes which occurred on the Continent, where an idle nobility scorned to dabble in business. In later centuries a certain snobbishness did set in against trade but Tudor England had the advantage of 'making gentlemen so easily', as a contemporary commented.

Books became more plentiful in Tudor households, thanks to the industry of William Caxton whose presses poured out a hundred books before the end of the fifteenth century. Popular titles were Aesop's *Fables*, [Thomas] Malory's *Morte d' Arthur* and the works of [Geoffrey] Chaucer. Printing also encouraged music-making in the home as songs and madrigals became more cheaply and easily available. Between 1588 and 1630 over eighty collections of songs by composers such as [Thomas] Morley, [John] Dowland and [Thomas] Campion were printed. Singing became so fashionable that it was an essential accomplishment for any gentleman. In 1597 Thomas Morley describes an embarrassing incident in his *Plaine and Easie Introduction to Practicale Musicke*:

Supper being ended, and musicke bookes (according to the custom) being brought to table, the mistresse of the house presented me with a part, earnestly requesting me to sing; but when, after many excuses, I protested unfainedly that I could not, every one began to wonder! Yes, some whispered to others, demanding how I was brought up; so that upon shame of mine ignorance, I goe now to seek out mine old friend Master Gnorimus to make myself his scholler.

Food

Food was a great pleasure to the people of Tudor England, as foreigners were quick to note. The Italian Andreas Franciscus described in 1497 how the common people 'delight in banquets and variety of meat and food, and they excel everyone in preparing them with an excessive abundance. They eat very frequently, at times more than is suitable, and are particularly fond of young swans, rabbits, deer and seabirds.' By common people he presumably meant citizens and yeomen, for there would have been no 'excessive abundance' in the homes of the labourers. Bread, bacon, cheese and beer or cider would have been the staple diet in a poor home, with meat once or twice a week if they were lucky.

Fifty years later the pleasures of the stomach had not grown less popular, according to a scornful Spaniard who accompanied Philip of Spain to the court of Queen Mary in 1554:

> There are no distractions here except eating and drinking, the only variety they understand. . . . There is plenty of beer here and they drink more than would fill the Valladolid river. In summer the ladies and some gentlemen put sugar in their wine, with the result that there are great goings on in the palace.

A new vegetable was introduced to English diet in the reign of Elizabeth—the potato, brought back from America by Sir Walter Raleigh. He had an estate in Ireland and the potato was first cultivated on a large scale there. On the whole the climate and the soil suited it, and 'Ireland's lazy root' became so much the staple diet that the failure of one year's crop could bring famine to the country. In England it made slower progress, was grown as a garden vegetable rather than as a field crop and was far more popular, to begin with, in the north than in the south. It is difficult now to imagine life without it.

Raleigh was also responsible for introducing into England the 'noxious weed' tobacco which he had observed giving pleasure to the natives of the New World. The habit caught on, but strictly for men only—who could imagine a woman with a clay pipe in her mouth? Men found the process soothing and companionable. It was not until the next reign that we find the first fulminations against smoking, written by King James himself: 'Herein is not only a great vanity, but a great contempt of God's good gifts, that the sweetness of man's breath . . . should be wilfully corrupted by this stinking smoke.' He imposed heavy duties on the import of tobacco for social as well as economic reasons.

Fashions

In fashion ostentation was the hallmark of the Tudor period. Never before and never again was such sheer extravagance seen in the way of clothes; the richest material was lavishly embroidered and studded with precious stones. Two dresses, one for each of his daughters, cost one doting father £1,500. (Few people have attempted an exact conversion scale, but this was at a time when a country mansion could be built for £5,000, and a man with an income of £40 a year was looked upon as a substantial citizen.) Critics of the day complained that women walked about with the worth of two manors around their necks. Unmarried women had a good deal of space upon which to display their jewels, for the custom of the day allowed virgins to expose their breasts; married women were expected to be rather more modest. Elizabeth Tudor, most admirable of women in many ways, was what one might call a professional virgin and took such advantage of this fashion that one shocked visitor reported that when she leaned forward he could practically see her navel.

Over a period of 118 years fashions altered, of course, but the general trend was towards a rigidity, an artificiality hitherto unknown. The medieval lady had nipped in her waist; by Elizabeth I's time women of fashion were nipping in their whole torsos and wearing bodices of which the narrow lowest point was almost on the pelvis. Below, from hip to heel, skirts spread wide, held out by stiffly starched petticoats, or a wire cage called a farthingale. It is fortunate that the appearance of these gorgeous if ridiculous clothes coincided with the development of portrait painting, which has left numerous dazzling records of Tudor fashions.

Men's clothes—for those who wished to be considered part of the fashionable world—were equally extravagant, with enormous sleeves and breeches stuffed with wool or bran, and that slightly obscene appendage the codpiece, jewelled and embroidered to draw attention to the wearer's virility. A man anxious to cut a dash at court would pawn an estate in order to buy an eye-taking jewel for his cap. . . .

The most extraordinary fashion of all was the ruff. It began with a standing collar, starched and edged with lace, and ended as a stiffly pleated wheel, in extreme cases fifteen inches in radius. This made eating difficult and there is mention of specially

Fashions were extravagant during the Elizabethan Age. Clothing for both men and women was made of rich, lavishly embroidered fabrics.

long-handled spoons. Men and married women could have their necks entirely encircled, but the maiden state must be proclaimed by keeping the throat and bosom exposed and wearing the ruff only as far forward as the shoulders. This upset its balance, and it had to be supported by struts of metal or whalebone. The ruffs were washed, dipped into a solution of flour and water and then pleated by the application of heated tongs. At the height of the fashion hundreds of women on the outskirts of London earned their bread by caring for ruffs, a process which demanded plenty of water, clean air and space for bleaching and drying. Piccadilly was one of these areas and is said to have taken its name from the business, though strictly speaking the term 'picadil' applied rather to a shoulder ornament than to the ruff.

Higher Standards of Living Achieved at Expense of Poor

The wealth which paid for the fine new houses, extravagant clothes and gargantuan meals came mainly from a more economic use of agricultural land, enabling the country to produce a surplus above the needs of subsistence, which fed the towns and was traded abroad. This was achieved by the enclosure of waste land, demesne land, common land or open-field strips into large arable fields or pasture for sheep. As a result many peasants (nearly all of them were now freemen) were evicted from their smallholdings, or lost their rights to the common land, and labourers were put out of work in the areas where enclosure for pasture took place for sheep farming required a smaller work force. The numbers concerned were small compared with those who were to suffer in the eighteenth-century enclosures, but to concerned observers it seemed as if a whole way of life was being broken up. Sir Thomas More protested that 'Sheep eateth men' and in his *Utopia* published in 1516 he described the fate of the peasant farmers:

> The husbandmen be thrust oute of their owne, or els either by coveyne and fraude, or by violent oppression they be put besydes it, or by wronges and injuries thei be so weried that they be compelled to sell all: by one means therfore or by other, either by hooke or crooke they must needes depart awaye, poore, selye, wretched soules.

The situation was not improved by the dissolution of the

monasteries in the reign of Henry VIII when nearly one-fifteenth of the countryside passed into the hands of new owners, concerned chiefly to enrich themselves and not bound by the medieval concept of responsibility for their tenants. The higher standard of living enjoyed by the majority of the population in Elizabeth's reign was therefore only achieved at the expense of many of the poorest class who were turned off the land. Some went to swell the towns, others to swell the new class of beggars and vagabonds. By the second half of the century the problem of poverty was so great that Parliament was forced to recognize it in the Poor Law which made parishes responsible for providing employment or subsistence for the unemployed.

The Role of Servants

Lu Emily Pearson

In Elizabethan society, a high proportion of the population worked in households as servants. Some estimates indicate that 25 percent of the population may have been servants at any given time. Servants were paid employees who lived with the family and often became members of their employer's household. In this excerpt from *Elizabethans at Home*, Lu Emily Pearson examines the role of servants and their contributions to the well-ordered household in Elizabethan society. Pearson spent many years teaching Shakespeare and Elizabethan literature to American college students as well as researching Elizabethan family relationships in England.

O ne means of determining the Elizabethan's social status was by the number of servants he kept, for servants in a way indicated gentility. In the homes of the privileged the number was likely to be large, and if so, they made quite an impressive appearance in bright new liveries when the master entertained important personages or when he was accompanied by them on a journey. In the early days of the Tudors the servants wore blue coats with the master's badge in silver on the left arm, but by the end of the century the coats were commonly trimmed with lace, and the color and ornament were determined by the family they served. Numbers of servants and the quality of their apparel, therefore, varied considerably during the age of Queen Elizabeth. . . .

Financial Drain

When Lord Burghley's fortunes were at their best, however, he was said to have eighty men in livery and the best men of England competing to enter his service. Twenty men served at his table, each being handsomely paid, though an ordinary servant's maximum wages were £5 per year. Like most Elizabethans, Burghley dined but twice a day, dinner at 11:00 in the morning, and supper at 6:00 in the evening. Regardless of whether he was at home, his entire household observed these hours, and breakfast was also provided for those who needed or desired it. His entertainment of the Queen and high officials and friends added much to his carefully calculated expenses. When Elizabeth visited him, he could hardly expect to entertain her for less than two to three thousand pounds, and this occurred a dozen times. When she visited Leicester at Kenilworth, the cost of entertaining her was over six thousand pounds. Among the items that ran high in the amusement provided by Leicester were the thirteen bears "worried by ban-dogs." He was said to have died £70,000 in debt to the Crown, but Burghley's careful management prevented any such disaster to his fortune, although his wealth was not so great as those hearing the reading of the will had expected it to be. . . .

The expenses of such households were a matter of much concern to English nobles. Though with careful management they might keep out of debt, at the same time some of their servants were rolling together little fortunes for themselves at their master's expense. Certainly the extensive scale in the lord's living would be a temptation to many menials. The Earl of Derby living "quietly" in the country at Latham in 1587 had more than a hundred servants to care for his household. His three officers (steward, comptroller, and receiver in general) had three servants each, and the master had seven gentlemen-in-waiting and a page. In 1590, the earl and his family of five had one hundred forty servants. When he served as ambassador to France in 1584, his retinue consisted of seventy regular attendants and sixty others. All had two liveries each, one of purple and gold lace and the other of black satin and taffeta, and all wore heavy gold chains. So great was the expense of this service abroad that he had to negotiate with Burghley for a loan of £1,000 from an alderman.

In spite of all the private and special hospitality they extended to visiting officials, the great lords in service to the Queen often preferred service at home to going abroad on embassies. Yet in spite of careful management they were fighting debt on one hand and trying to make a suitable impression on the other. After twenty years of service to the Queen, the Earl of Huntingdon died in debt to the Crown for £20,000. Raleigh's services left him "comparatively" poor in spite of special favors in monopolies, etc.

Sir Philip Sidney's father sacrificed far more than he gained for all his labors, and he was well known for the excellent management of his resources. An impressive appearance made it next to impossible to break away from the parade of servants so well established by the 1560's. Though the young Earl of Oxford was often referred to as extravagant, he was not accused of making an ostentatious display of respect for his father by returning from the funeral attended by one hundred forty men all in mourning apparel. So strong was the general pride in "great place," however, that most Elizabethans in high office were not averse to their appointments even though they must expect as a result heavy drains upon their financial resources.

Household Discipline

All well-regulated households were under strict discipline, but establishments of great lords must be under very strict control if there was to be any order at all. To maintain smooth functioning in all the offices, there were rules similar to those drawn up by John Harrington for the master of a household:

> A servant must not be absent from morning or evening meals or prayers without excuse lest he be fined twopence each time.
>
> Any servant late to dinner would be fined twopence.
>
> Any man waiting at table without a trencher in his hand, except for good excuse, would be fined one penny.
>
> The court gate must be kept closed during a meal.
>
> Any man leaving a door open he had found shut would be fined one penny unless he could show good cause.
>
> Any man going to the kitchen without reasonable excuse would be fined one penny, and the cook would be fined one penny also.
>
> Any man provoking another to strike or striking another would be liable to dismissal.
>
> For each oath, a servant would be fined one penny.
>
> For a dirty shirt on Sunday or a missing button, the fine would be six pence.
>
> After 8:00 A.M. no bed must be found unmade and no fireplace or candle box left unclean, or the fine would be one penny.

The hall must be cleaned in an hour.

All guests' rooms must be tidied within four hours after the departure of the guests.

The whole house must be swept and dusted each Friday.

The fines collected by deductions from wages for infraction of the above rules were bestowed upon the poor. Although the rising hour in such rules was given as six in winter and five in summer, in most great households servants rose from five to seven in winter and four to six in summer. Retiring hours were correspondingly early, for the poor light given by candles made it necessary for them to engage in most of their labor during daylight.

The household discipline naturally depended to a great extent upon the master's force of character, for he was nominally the head of the establishment even though his wife usually controlled the maidservants. Commands or a box on the ear would keep most servants obedient, but it was not unusual for both master and mistress to punish servants severely, especially when they conducted themselves in a childish or impudent manner. Some Elizabethans, therefore, thrashed maidservants as well as menservants when they misbehaved. Naturally the treatment of servants became a subject of discussion for preachers and moralists and all writers of domestic literature, for servants were no small problem in some of the homes. Pious authors admonished both masters and mistresses to remember that their own relation to God was that of servant to master, and to treat their servants fairly and justly.

Since it was customary to expect servants to stay for life in an established household, the relationship between them and their masters was often familiar and affectionate. Sometimes the relationship took on the paternal character, and many times, in the homes of country people especially, the servers were looked upon as members of the family and regarded fondly like the children. In such cases, servants in both town and country houses were chastened gently or severely when they did wrong, and praised when they were good. More was expected of them than of children, of course, especially in the way of loyalty. It may be that the discipline to which they were subject in well-ordered homes and the humility expected of them made them more attached to their masters than they would have been had the demands of good service and proper deference been at all slack. Most masters and mistresses at the head of a respectful household won their servants' love and fidelity; in return, they tried to the best of their ability to live up to their responsibility for those who served them and lived with them under the same roof. . . .

Relationships Between Master and Servant

Dismissals after long service were frowned on by good masters. Sir Robert Sidney, for example, usually permitted his wife to manage the household servants, but when she wished to dismiss one who had been in their employ for years, he wrote her tactfully yet firmly that the man must not be cast off in his old age. "If he have offended you, he shall ask your forgiveness, and you shall remit the offence to me," he said, and added, "A chamber also I will have him for himself in the house. But it is not my meaning he should keep any family there.". . .

Where to draw the line between easy, friendly relations between master and servant was most important because the comparative lack of privacy in the home made it necessary to keep servants in their place if there was to be any harmony. This was particularly true of personal servants. At the same time the lack of privacy made it necessary to maintain easy relations lest there develop a strained attitude that in itself would be intolerable. . . .

Assigned Duties

Each servant in a stable household had his appointed task and, when well trained and attached to a house of distinction, performed his duties with pride and usually with genuine devotion. The lady's maid in such a home might come from a family of social distinction, who had placed her in service to learn how to be a great lady herself. The women in waiting to an important lady must have gentle blood in their veins in order to qualify for the honor of serving such a mistress. In this same household there might also be several men from families of gentle blood, their duties being commensurate with their social position or as preparation for a master's duties in case fortune brought them such responsibilities. . . .

In large establishments, the chamberlain was in charge of the master's room. Like the lady's maid, he must keep himself clean and neat at all times and serve his lord cheerfully and courteously with much ceremonious bowing. He saw that his master's linen was clean and warmed at the fire before being put on. He took care also that the fire did not smoke. When his master was ready to rise, the chamberlain placed a cushioned chair before the fire with a cushion for the lord's feet and a cloth to lay over his feet to keep them warm. When, either alone or with the help of other servants under his direction, he had dressed his lord in tunic, doublet stomacher, short and long hose, and shoes, he trussed the hose as high as the lord wished them, and then placed a kerchief around his master's shoulders to protect his clothes while his hair was combed. His master was then given warm water in which to wash his face and hands. This done, the servant kneeled and asked the lord what robe he wished to wear, and later, having helped him into it, got the girdle and fastened it, and ceremoniously brought his hood or cap or hat and cloak or cape. Before the lord left the chamber, the servant inspected him well, and brushed off all possible lint or dust. . . .

With all this careful division of labor among well-trained servants, the duties involved in serving a meal were many and complicated. Minor details were superintended by butler, carver, and server. It was the butler's duty to keep special well-sharpened knives provided for chopping loaves of bread, preparing these loaves for the table, and making trenchers when bread was used for this purpose. The lord's bread and that of his family might be cut from new loaves, but all other bread used by the household was one to three days old. When used for trenchers, bread had to be four days old. Lords who owned fine plate never used bread for trenchers unless unusual circumstances required them to do so; such might be a sudden and totally unexpected number of guests that had to be dined. Most of the bread was baked in small, individual loaves that were broken at will by individuals at table. If the loaves were too brown or had oven grit on them, the butler was well reprimanded for his carelessness. In ordinary homes, each person scraped his own little loaf. . . .

Besides the many menials and the supervisors in the kitchen there was the kitchen clerk, who was in charge of the meals, directed the dressing of all meats, and measured out the supplies.

So valuable were the spices that he took charge of them himself. He even determined the scale of wages for the grooms and yeomen of some households, and ordered the general household clothing. Thus the kitchen clerk was often accountable for some of the important expenditures in home maintenance. The cutler or bladesmith was responsible for sharp edges on the kitchen knives; the pantler supervised the pantry and assisted the butler or assumed all the duties of that office. The cellarer or steward of wines had an important position, for he and the butler must see that the drink for the master and his household was safe and agreeable. The chief cook had charge of the other cooks and the scullions, among whom might be extra help during feasts when the kitchen was likely to be the busiest and noisiest place in the entire household.

Kitchen servants were expected to dine on the remains from the lord's table or to cook simple food for themselves. At feasts they were sure of generous amounts of rich food, but at other times all servants were expected to dine simply, under the watchful eye of the kitchen clerk. Scraps from their table also went to the beggars at the gate, and the almoner saw that "broken meats" from all the tables were gathered at the end of a meal to be given to charity. They were often worth waiting for, as the huge pies with walls several inches thick, molded to resemble a building or an animal, were filled with ham, veal, and large balls of forcemeat. The highly seasoned meat of the latter was even worth fighting for if the beggars were clamorous for food. . . .

The influence of the family upon the servants was much stronger when servants became actual members of the family, as so often occurred in Elizabethan establishments. Thus the stress placed upon the need of good and kind household management on the part of husband and wife resulted more often than not in such close ties that the master was frequently his brother-servant's keeper, and the wife, the good angel of her maids.

Elizabethan Travel at Home

M. St. Clare Byrne

The following essay is taken from *Elizabethan Life in Town and Country* by British author M. St. Clare Byrne. Originally published in 1925, the book promptly became an accepted authority for the social history of the Elizabethan Age. One reviewer described the book as having "almost every sentence based on contemporary sources." Using historical research, Byrne presents a picture of Elizabethan society and its habits of thought and modes of living, including travel. Travel was dangerous as well as arduous, yet travel was an important part of Elizabethan life and economy. Byrne points out that although some Elizabethans never left their local villages, some livelihoods required ongoing travel. For the most part, Elizabethans still used roads made by the Romans.

To travel, for an Elizabethan, did not always mean to arrive, but it usually meant to adventure, for the risks of the road were many. Travelling was an arduous undertaking and much might befall a man before he came to his journey's end. The highway itself was an ideal right of passage rather than a substantial track giving solid footing to man and beast. It is scarcely an exaggeration to say that, judged by modern standards, roads were almost nonexistent. The four great Roman highways and their dependent roads remained, but apart from these there were only customary tracks across the country, often impassable in winter, rutted and uneven in summer. The wise traveller guided his horse off the beaten pathway, and cantered alongside, on the edge of somebody's field. No one could deliberately travel for pleasure; people took to the road when it was necessary to get from one place to another, and men travelled about their business. Even in the towns, moreover, the streets were generally in a worse condition than the average farm track is today. Roads

M. St. Clare Byrne, *Elizabethan Life in Town and Country*. London: Methuen & Co., Ltd., 1961.

were not made; they happened, because a sufficient number of people and horses trod out a track.

The Roman roads had carried the traffic of the Middle Ages, its trade and its pilgrimages, with the help of newer cross-roads and bypaths which were more or less kept up by the manor. With the suppression of the old religion and the gradual decay of the manorial system in the late fifteenth and early sixteenth centuries the roads became less generally used and were allowed to fall into a hopeless state of disrepair. Bridges were left to become ruinous, holes and ruts were mended with a few faggots and some brushwood which looked substantial enough but often created a veritable death-trap for man and horse. The Kentish roads leading from the ports to the capital were probably as good as any in the kingdom; nevertheless they were described in Henry VIII's reign as passable only at 'great pains, peril, and jeopardy'. When the wayfaring life of the Middle Ages came to an end the roads of the country began to fall into a state of decay which was not arrested till the reign of Mary Tudor.

Efforts to Repair Roads

In 1555 a statute for amending the highways described them as "very noisome and tedious to travel in and dangerous to all passengers and carriages." The statute was a memorable one, because by it the responsibility for the repair of the roads was apportioned. Hitherto it had been possible for a locality to avoid collision with the law by the most inadequate or perfunctory repairs. The provision of the necessary funds had been left to anybody or nobody. Bequests in wills occasionally furnished the necessary gravel or stones for repairs, but they had become less frequent in the sixteenth century, and taxation was applied to many purposes, but not to this. In 1555, however, the responsibility for providing the necessary funds, materials, tools, and labour was definitely laid upon each parish in the kingdom and upon each of its inhabitants. They had to choose one of their number each year to be their Surveyor of Highways; the richer members of the community had then, when called upon, to furnish him with teams and men for the work; the poorer sort had to give their labour for eight hours a day on four consecutive days.

The reform was thus more or less adequately begun, and the

office of Surveyor thus created must have been quite one of the most unpleasant that could fall to the lot of any good Tudor citizen. It was an age in which there was no lack of public spirit amongst high or low, but it must have taken a very considerable amount of it to prevent the relations between the unfortunate surveyor and his neighbours from being anything but strained. To be compelled, under penalty of a forty shilling fine for neglect of duty, to make the whole village turn out and mend the roads, when perhaps every second individual ought to have been working on his own holding, was no happy task for any man. Refusal of the office, however, was no solution of the difficulty for most people, as that cost no less than five pounds; and refusal of work was no solution for those called upon, as that meant an appearance before the Justice and a fine . . . so the roads of England began to be more or less continually, if amateurishly, repaired, and the actual passageway became a little safer than it had been. In theory the method would appear a sufficient one, but upon the practical results [William] Harrison, as usual, has some illuminating remarks. 'The intent of the statute', he admits, 'is very profitable', but in practice the rich evade their share, and the poor so loiter in their labour that scarcely two good days' work gets accomplished. Individual surveyors, too, had a habit of mending the lanes and ways that led to their own pastures, instead of concentrating upon the highway.

Fifty years later complaint was still loud. Thomas Procter in 1607 reports that there was a great lack of good roads, 'to the daily continual great grief and heartbreaking of man and beast, with charges, hindrances, wearing and tiring of them, and sometimes to the great and imminent danger of their lives, and often spoil and loss of goods'. Procter was a sensible and practical man, and from his recommendations we realize that since the Romans made their great ways nobody had bothered either to lay any foundations for the English roads or to drain them. 'One principal and chief cause of all bad and foul ways is that the rain water or other water doth lie and rest upon the highways (not orderly and soundly made) which with the working of cart wheels and others, doth pierce down more deeper into the said ways, and so more and more doth soften and rot the same'. Not only did travellers in their desire to find a fair track ride through the fields to the 'great hurt and spoil of fences and grounds with riding and going on the corn', but in some places they would refuse to use an old highway at all, as in the case of the road that once led from Gray's Inn to High Barnet. This, Norden tells us, 'was refused of wayfaring men and carriers by reason of the deepness and dirty passage in the winter season', so that a new way had to be laid through the park of the Bishop of London from Highgate Hill direct to Whetstone, for the use of which all travellers as they passed through the gate on Highgate Hill paid toll to the Bishop. Foreigners were equally emphatic in their condemnation. Frederick Duke of Würtemberg, for example, who travelled from Oxford to Cambridge in 1592, does not mince matters: 'On the road we passed through a villainous boggy and wild country, and several times missed our way, because the country thereabouts is very little inhabited and is nearly a waste, and there is one spot in particular where the mud is so deep that . . . it would scarcely be possible to pass with a coach in winter or rainy weather'.

Highway Robbers

Besides the ruts and the mire and the ruinous bridges there were other dangers which threatened the life and the property of the Elizabethan traveller. In the belts of forest which so often surrounded the cultivated areas lurked highway robbers ready to hold up the solitary rider or even a small company of travellers. Generally the victims would escape with their lives, sometimes not; the penalty for highway robbery was the same as for highway murder, and with the gallows ready for either offence there was no particular reason why the gentleman of the road, the 'High Lawyer', should restrict himself solely to the former, if he happened to lose his temper with an unwilling or stout-hearted prize.

Gadshill, near Rochester, the scene of Falstaff's[1] exploit with the men in buckram, was long notorious as the resort of highway robbers. Shooter's Hill near Blackheath was another danger zone for the traveller, as were the deserted stretches of Salisbury Plain and Newmarket Heath. Prudent men made haste to reach

1. Falstaff is a character in Shakespeare's *King Henry IV*.

their destination before nightfall involved them in a passage perilous; Shakespeare himself must often, as a 'lated traveller', have 'spurred apace to reach the timely inn' while 'the west yet glimmered with some streaks of day'. A French conversation manual of the time, in one of its 'familiar talks', gives as a matter of course the following picture of the perils of the road; one of the travellers wishes for a guide to conduct them as the way is so dangerous, and they overtake a horseman and inquire their right road. He replies that they have not far to go, but that the way is 'very tedious to keep, furthermore it is so dirty and miry that your horse will be therein to the girths'. They tip a poor ploughman for leading them to the village, and before they dismiss him the following conversation ensues:

> *Traveller.* I pray you set me a little in my right way out of the village.
>
> *Ploughman.* Keep still the right hand until you come to the corner of a wood, then turn at the left hand.
>
> *Traveller.* Have we no thieves at that forest?
>
> *Ploughman.* No, sir, for the provost-marshal hung the other day a half dozen at the gallows which you see before you at the top of that hill.
>
> *Traveller.* Truly I fear lest we be here robbed . . . we shall spur a little harder for it waxeth night.

The "Great and Sumptuous" Inns

On arrival at the inn, however, a good reception awaited such travellers. The next dialogue shows them welcomed by the mistress of the house, who promises that they shall want for nothing. Their horses are handed over to the ostler [horse caretaker] for a rub down and a 'bottle of hay', and the gentleman enter the inn-chamber where they call for sack and for a man to pull off their riding boots. Upstairs in the bedroom Jane the chambermaid is kindling a fire and getting her warming pan ready, clean sheets are being put upon the feather bed, and everyone is bustling round to provide for the new arrivals that good cheer for which the English inns were famous.

The inns in the towns which lay on the great main roads, so Harrison tells us, were 'great and sumptuous'. 'Every man', he asserts, 'may use his inn as his own house in England'. He has special praise for the napery, the bedding, and the tapestry, and assures us that 'each comer is sure to lie in clean sheets, wherein no man hath been lodged since they came from the laundress'. Some of these inns seem to have been able to lodge over a hundred people—three hundred, according to Harrison—'and their horses at ease, and thereto with a very short warning make such provision for their diet as to him that is unacquainted therewithall may seem to be incredible'. In some of the large towns there were 'twelve or sixteen such inns at the least', each with a brightly painted signboard which Harrison condemns as a costly vanity. 'It is a world', he exclaims, 'to see how each owner of them contendeth with other for goodness of entertainment of their guests, as about fineness and change of linen, furniture of bedding, beauty of rooms, service at the table, costliness of plate, strength of drink, variety of wines, or well using of horses'.

While a traveller sojourned in his house the master of the inn held himself responsible for his guest's belongings: 'If he lose aught whilst he abideth in the inn the host is bound by a general custom to restore the damage, so that there is no greater security any where for travellers'. On the other hand, however, Harrison admits that the inn servants, and the ostlers and tapsters were often in league with gangs of highwaymen. They had many sly ways of discovering whether a man was a likely prize or not.

When a traveller arrived and dismounted from his horse the ostler would busily take down the capcase (or travelling bag) from the saddle-bow, judging by its weight whether the contents were worth robbing. If the ostler failed in his plan, then the man who saw to the guest's chamber would make his attempt, moving the bag ostensibly to a more convenient position in the room; and 'the tapster . . . doth mark his behaviour, and what plenty of money he draweth when he payeth the shot . . . so that it shall be an hard matter to escape all their subtle practises'. Then the word would be conveyed to their purse-cutting confederates 'to the utter undoing of many an honest yeoman as he journeyeth by the way'.

Conveyances of the Road

Travelling, as we have thus seen, had its manifold dangers; it had also its fatigues. Those who could take to the road on foot were perhaps the luckiest; horses meant speed, but the saddles of those days were small and hard and so uncomfortable for a heavy rider that one distinguished foreigner—that Duke of Würtemberg, who complained of our villainous boggy ways—actually took one home with him as a curiosity. Women frequently travelled on horseback, either riding on a pillion or else on a man's saddle. Coaches were sometimes used for long journeys, but these too must have been extremely tiring as they had no springs to them, the body of the coach resting directly on the axles. The jolting and the jarring must have been intolerable, but for anyone with a family of womenfolk to transport, these lumbering conveyances were both convenient and cheap, and during this reign they came more and more into favour. In spite of the discomfort the Queen herself frequently used a coach for travelling, and so set the fashion for others of her sex. It even became possible, according to Fynes Moryson in 1607, to hire a coach for journeys near London at the rate of ten shillings a day.

Carts, both two-wheeled and four-wheeled, were used by the country-people for transporting their goods and farm produce. They were also necessary for the moving of a large household, or for the Queen's annual progresses. On such occasions as these latter the roads must have been churned into an even worse state of mud and ruts than usual by the long train of wagons required to carry the goods and provisions which accompanied each stage of the journey. Harrison comments on the fact that sumpter horses had been given up in his time, because 'Our Princes and the Nobility have their carriage commonly made by carts, whereby it cometh to pass that when the Queen's Majesty doth remove from any place to another there are usually 400 carewares which amount to the sum of 2,400 horses appointed out of the countries adjoining, whereby her carriage is conveyed safely unto the appointed place'.

The regular frequenters of the road were the posts and the carriers. The latter during this reign began to use carts as well as horses, and would occasionally carry passengers besides goods. The service was a well-organized and regular one; the great towns all had their carriers, who kept them in communication with London. . . .

Rogues of the Open Road

By Elizabeth's time vagabondage had increased to such an alarming extent that the regulation of it was one of the chief problems with which the Government was confronted. The wandering beggars numbered in their ranks all kinds of men and women, from the real gipsies—the Romanys—to the impotent poor and the sturdy rascals whose one aim in life was to avoid honest work. Amongst them was many a "wild rogue", vagabond by birth, born to the road, and sometimes boastful of three such generations behind him. Discharged serving-men, old soldiers, ruined small-holders, out-of-work agricultural labourers, masterless men of all kinds helped to make up an almost unbelievably numerous crew of rascals, who swarmed over the whole countryside practising the gentle art of living on nothing a year at the expense of the respectable members of the community.

The most fantastic and horrible of these creatures to be met on the high road were the Palliards, the Abraham-Men, and the Counterfeit Cranks. The Palliard, who was also known in the canting tongue as a Clapperdudgeon, was the kind of beggar who deliberately covered his limbs with loathsome running sores to rouse compassion and elicit alms. To make these raw and bleeding places they would tie arsenic or ratsbane on an ankle or an arm. When it had produced its corrosive effect they would then leave the sore exposed, and surround it with bloody and filthy rags, and so take their way from fair to fair and market to market, sometimes obtaining as much as five shillings a week in charity. Sham 'old soldiers' used much the same method to produce 'wounds', applying unslaked lime, soap, and iron rust, which made the arm appear black, while the sore was 'raw and reddish but white about the edges like an old wound' [wrote Thomas Dekker].

The Counterfeit Crank was another rogue who also dressed himself in the filthiest rags imaginable, daubed his face with blood, and pretented to have the falling sickness or some other dreadful affliction. One of the favourite tricks in his repertoire was to fall grovelling in the dirt at the feet of a passer-by, counterfeiting froth at the mouth by judicious sucking of a piece of soap! [Thomas] Harman tells us in his Caveat of one such rogue who earned fourteen and three-pence halfpenny in a day.

The Abraham-Man was perhaps the most terrifying figure of the three, as he pretended to be mad. Tom o' Bedlam and Poor Tom were other names for him. These impostors roamed the country half-naked. 'He walketh bare armed and bare legged,' [John] Awdelay tells us, 'and carrieth a pack of wool or a stick with bacon on it or such like a toy'.

A disreputable life they led, these rascals of the highway, but merry enough, so long as they achieved their main object, which was the avoidance of work in any shape or form. The Anglers amongst them would fish for linen off the hedges and trifles from inside a room with an open window, their tackle consisting of a long stick with a hook at the end of it. The Prigger of Prancers had an eye for a good nag, and woe to the farmer who left his horse loose in a meadow when one of these rogues was about. The Rufflers ruffled it after the manner of their kind, begging from the able-bodied, openly robbing the unprotected. The Rogue would put his hand to anything, picking the pockets of poor fools like Perdita's brother, turning ballad-monger or pedlar or pilferer as occasion served. And at the head of their profession, chiefs of the gang, were the Upright Men, who being the strongest and most influential members of the vagabond community not only had their choice amongst the women but frequently lived by extorting contributions from members of their own lower orders.

Entertainers and Peddlers Roamed the Highways

More or less identified with this motley throng of beggars and their wenches were the minstrels, pedlars, tinkers, and bearwards, fortune-tellers and jugglers. They too led the vagabond life, roaming up and down the highways and frequenting the country fairs. The minstrels fiddled on the village given, in the streets, outside the ale-houses, singing their 'bawdy songs, filthy ballads, and scurvy rhymes' whenever they could gather an audience. Often enough the pedlars and tinkers used their apparent trades merely as a protection—many of them were as ready as any Rogue or Ruffler to 'work' their way by thieving and trickery. The bearwards, with their half-savage beasts, added a real terror to life for the country children; the jugglers and the fortune-tellers awed and thrilled the country audiences with their legerdemain and their prognostications. Rascals all of them, disturbers of the peace, enemies of law and order, they were none of them pleasant companions for an honest and prosperous citizen as he trotted his comfortable cob along the Queen's highway. The fraternity of the open road constituted perhaps the most pressing social problem of the day, and the traveller had little chance to overlook it.

In Society: Politics, Religion, Marriage and Family, Education

CHAPTER

2

Chapter Preface

Queen Elizabeth influenced every aspect of society during her reign of almost unprecedented length and prosperity. Historian A.H. Dodd describes the queen's personal character and influence on the age that bears her name:

> The whole age is coloured by the rich personality of the queen herself, but never swamped by it: one of her triumphs was the active response she drew from a wide range of social levels and geographical areas, making her reign equally an age of the ordinary Englishman. For what elicited the response was devotion not so much to the abstract concept of England as to a living person, seen through a haze of romance yet decidedly human and accessible.

Elizabeth's popularity was enhanced by her actions to benefit England's poor. Elizabeth's Poor Laws were the first legislation to make the poor the government's responsibility. For example, one of the laws mandated that government give work to the poor to allow them to live on a subsistence level. Elizabeth also took steps to solve a long-standing conflict between Catholics and Protestants that tore at the very foundation of society. The queen decided to influence Parliament to pass the Acts of Settlement in 1559, making the Church of England Protestant once more.

Another example of the queen's influence occurred on the fashion scene. Perhaps in no age has there been such great extravagance of apparel than in Elizabeth's reign. Many portraits show the queen decked out in silks and satins, brocades, velvets, and jewels. She was definitely a style setter. Ladies from the middle classes to the nobility mimicked her dress, hairstyles, and makeup. In order to resemble their queen, fashionable ladies dyed their hair in shades of gold to red and used makeup to achieve an alabaster skin look. Historian William Stearns Davis wrote that even yeomen "think nothing of flaunting silks, velvets, damasks, and taffetas if they can find the . . . credit to obtain them." It has been said "such was the inordinate love of gay apparel amongst all classes that many a gallant preferred to prank it in his silks and velvets rather than to the spend thrift gallant . . . is at length starving himself on three-penny dinners in order to make an astonishing show with his cloak, ruff, and doublet."

The queen had an uncanny ability to inspire and influence the nobility as well as ordinary people. Her famous Royal Progresses across the English countryside were designed to project a favorable image of the queen to her public in the days before instant communication. Under the guidance of Queen Elizabeth, England evolved from a medieval state into a modern nation.

The Queen and the People

Christopher Haigh

Throughout her reign, Queen Elizabeth cultivated the common touch. Love for her subjects was a recurring theme in her speeches and in the work of her image makers. Christopher Haigh the author of *Elizabeth I*, from which the following essay is taken, explores Queen Elizabeth's relations with the people during her forty-five years on the throne. Haigh is a lecturer in modern history at Christ Church, Oxford University. He specializes in English religious and political history from 1509 to 1642.

E lizabeth I was a woman in danger: from the beginning of her reign to the end, she faced plots and rumours of plots. Some of the conspiracies posed real threats to her throne and to her life. In 1569, some of the leaders of the Revolt of the Northern Earls planned to remove Elizabeth and make Mary Stuart queen. In 1571, the Florentine banker Roberto Ridolfi hatched an elaborate scheme involving a Spanish invasion from the Netherlands, an English rebellion raised by the Duke of Norfolk, and the deposition of Elizabeth: the Pope, Philip II, and Norfolk were willing enough to help, and Elizabeth was saved only by the reluctance of the Spanish commander in the Netherlands and by Ridolfi's weakness for bragging to everyone what a wonderful plot he was organising. In 1583, Francis Throckmorton was the link man in a conspiracy to synchronise a French Catholic invasion with a rising of English Catholics, to free Mary Queen of Scots and make her queen of England. In 1586 a group of young Catholic fanatics swore to kill Elizabeth, and again planned to make Mary queen with foreign assistance. In 1599, the Essex circle formulated various schemes to seize Elizabeth, to make her the pawn of their faction, and force her to name James VI as heir. . . .

In 1583 the Warwickshire Catholic, John Somerville, told his neighbours he was going to shoot Elizabeth, and set off for London—but he declared his intention to everyone he met on the way and was arrested. . . .

With much jurisdiction, Elizabeth and her councillors feared for her safety. After all, in 1570 the Pope had declared the Queen excommunicate, and absolved her subjects from obedience to her. In 1584, after Somerville and Throckmorton, and the successful assassination of William of Orange in the Netherlands, the Council organized a Protestant vigilante group, the 'Bond of Association', pledged by oath to protect the Queen's life and, if they failed, to hunt down and murder her killers. The Privy Council drew up an 'Instrument of an Association for the preservation of the Queen's Majesty's royal person', and Secretary Walsingham supervised the distribution of copies to lords lieutenant and reliable magnates across the country. These local leaders then put the oath of membership to the leading gentry, and collected signatures for the Bond. It was a panic measure at a panic time, but the fear of disaster remained strong. In her last years, Elizabeth slept with a rusty old sword by her bed, and she made a bit of a fool of herself stalking around the Privy Chamber with the weapon, stabbing at curtains in case assassins lurked.

Nor was it simply a danger of assassination plots: there was a risk of rebellion. In 1597 Elizabeth told the French ambassador that 'she had to deal with nobles of divers humours, and peoples who, although they made great demonstration of love towards her, nevertheless were fickle and inconstant, and she had to fear everything'. Some of her councillors agreed. One of the arguments used against expensive land wars in the 1590s was that heavier war taxation and military recruitment would lead to widespread popular disorder. . . . So Elizabeth pursued a propaganda policy designed to maximise popular loyalty to herself—not just because she liked to be cheered (though she certainly did), but because it was politically sensible. If she could attract the intense loyalty of ordinary people, then they might serve as a protection against assassination attempts—they would be on the lookout for critics of the regime, and might turn in any who posed a threat. A loyal nation would be less likely to rebel in hard times, and might more readily pay taxes and serve in royal armies and fleets. So Elizabeth did not only have to present sophisticated and allusive images of female rule to her educated courtiers; she had to present a simpler, more basic message to ordinary people. Somehow, the townspeople and peasants of England had to be made to love her.

A Public Queen

Some of Elizabeth's work was done for her. The clergy in their churches read out prayers for the Queen's safety and preached sermons on God's favour towards her; the judges at assizes warned of the need for vigilance against the enemies of the state; the sheriffs read out statutes and proclamations which stressed the need for order and obedience. But these tactics sought an allegiance which was passive and formal: a more fervent and active devotion to the royal person was needed if she was to be really safe. Elizabeth had to show herself to her people, and gain their adoration. In London, it was easy enough: from the beginning of the reign to the end, Elizabeth paraded in splendour through the streets and sailed on the Thames where her people could see her. On St George's Day 1559, a great spectacle was staged on the Thames, in which the Queen's barge was rowed up and down, escorted by a flotilla of boats and observed by large crowds on the banks; there was music and artillery salutes, and, in the evening, a firework display.

Elizabeth was very much a public queen. She always appeared in public for her Accession Day celebrations, which were usually associated with an elaborate procession through London before the splendid jousting in the tilt-yard. Even on 17 November 1602, when she was 69 and there was suspicion of an assassination attempt, she merely changed her route to avoid the danger and appeared much as scheduled. It is clear that the Queen always made a great impression on her subjects. Bishop Goodman, years after the event, remembered how, as a boy of 5 in 1588, he had seen Elizabeth one night at Whitehall. On news that the Queen was coming, he and his friends had run through the streets, to join the crowd shouting 'God save your Majesty' as she passed by in torchlight. 'God bless you all, my good people', she had replied, and the crowds were made to feel they really were blessed and they were truly her good people.

Away from London, of course, it was much more difficult for

the Queen to establish a rapport with the common people, but her regular summer progresses provided some opportunity. Elizabeth and her Court usually went on a ten-week summer progress. . . . Historians usually think of progresses in the context of Elizabeth's relations with nobility and gentry, but they were also occasions for the Queen to show herself to ordinary people as she crossed the countryside at a sedate pace. . . .

By the 1580s there was apparently a huge demand for images of the Queen: as well as the wholesale copying of portraits, the lower end of the patriotic market was now being catered for. Just as Elizabeth's courtiers began to wear jewelled cameos of the Queen, so her poorer subjects could acquire base-metal medallions to wear as expressions of loyalty. In the 1580s, too, woodcuts and engravings of Elizabeth became more common in books, and in the next decade many separate printed pictures were produced for sale. But the more widely the royal image was displayed, the more important controls became. There appears to have been some official decision in about 1594 that Elizabeth should be pictured as eternally youthful, presumably to prevent fears for the future. Although the face of the famous 'Ditchley portrait' became a pattern for the rest of the reign, in the copies it was rejuvenated into the softer face of a young woman. In 1596, the Privy Council ordered officials to seek out and destroy all unseemly portraits, which were said to have caused the Queen great offence: the object of the campaign seems to have been the elimination of the image of Elizabeth as an old woman, and engravings which showed her age appear to have been destroyed.

Those of Elizabeth's subjects who could not buy her picture might at least learn simple ballads of loyalty. The ballads were both unofficial propaganda weapons and opportunities for individuals to share by singing in public devotion to the Queen. There were love-songs to Elizabeth, as in the 1559

Come over the born, Bessy,
Come over the born, Bessy,
Sweet Bessy come over to me;
And I shall thee take,
And my dear lady make
Before all other that ever I see.

As the reign wore on, there were ballads in the form of hymns of thanks to God for Elizabeth's rule and her achievements. . . .

By the 1590s, however, the technique had changed. Until then, the ballads had usually related to real events, and given thanks for the Queen's accession or her continuing safety. But in her last decade, as the war dragged on, taxes grew more burdensome, food prices soared, and living standards fell, the ballad-writers ignored the facts and resorted to the 'big lie'. In the midst of war and growing poverty, the peace and prosperity of the reign were celebrated: 'A joyful new ballad of our queen's going to the parliament, showing her most happy and prosperous reign and the great care she hath for the government of her people, made this year 1593; 'A triumphant new ballad in honour of the queen's Majesty and her most happy government, who hath reigned in great prosperity thirty-seven years' and 'England's triumph, containing divers of those abundant blessings wherewith this our realm hath been blessed by our most gracious Queen Elizabeth's reign' in 1595. In many ballads, and especially in those published late in the reign, the emphasis was upon Elizabeth's care for her people, her motherly concern for the welfare of all her subjects and for the poor in particular. There was a deliberate attempt to project Elizabeth as the Queen of the poor, as the protectress of all those who carried the burdens of society. It was, of course, government by illusion. . . .

It was all heady stuff—and the people believed it. Perhaps Elizabeth did too.

The Queen's approach was much the same on progress, when she deliberately sought the affection of her subjects in public and well-publicised gestures. The Spanish ambassador, who travelled with her on the progress through Berkshire in 1568, reported that the Queen ordered her carriage into the thickest parts of the crowds, and stood up to wave and thank them for their welcome: 'She was received with great acclamations and signs of joy, as is customary in this country; whereat she was extremely pleased and told me so, giving me to understand how beloved she was by her subjects'. Elizabeth informed the ambassador that 'she attributed it all to God's miraculous goodness' but in fact the enthusiasm was the product of her own hard work and that of her propagandists. In 1572, on progress through Oxfordshire, Elizabeth sheltered from the rain in a barn; there, an old woman told her that the copyhold on the family's small farm was about to run out, so the Queen got her Council to write to the landlord asking him to extend the tenancy. The story soon spread—with help from the Council.

The Queen's Love for Her Subjects

These were practical ways in which Elizabeth tried to demonstrate her love for her subjects, and the loving relationship between queen and people was a regular theme in her own speeches and in the work of her image-makers. She appears to have worked on the assumption that if she boasted of her devotion often enough, she would never have to do anything about it—and if she told her people often enough how much they loved her, they would actually do it. The theme of loving care was set out by Lord Keeper Bacon in the first parliamentary speech of the reign: the Queen would not rule selfishly, but in ways which would meet the needs of her people—she was a princess 'to whom nothing—what nothing?—no, no worldly thing under the sun is so dear as the hearty love and goodwill of her nobles and subjects'. In 1563 Elizabeth herself promised to be a 'natural mother' to the realm; in 1589 she told a parliamentary delegation of her 'great and inestimable loving care towards her loving subjects: yea, more than of her own self, or than any of them have of themselves'. . . .

Outside Parliament, too, Elizabeth's subjects were reminded of the mutual love of queen and people. Her speech to the army at Tilbury in 1588 is justly famous:

> I have always so behaved myself that, under God, I have placed my chiefest strength and safeguard in the loyal hearts and good will of my subjects; and therefore I am come amongst you, as you see, at this time, not for my recreation and disport, but being resolved, in the midst and heat of the battle, to live or die amongst you all, to lay down for my God, and for my kingdom, and for my people, my honour and blood, even in the dust. . . .

The Queen had a strong, almost mystical, sense of personal identity with her people. She bragged to foreign ambassadors about how much her subjects loved her, and, in a private prayer of about 1579, she gave thanks that 'The love of my people hath appeared firm, and the devices of mine enemies frustrate'. But Elizabeth I was a realistic politician, who took few chances. She knew this support could not be taken for granted, and that she had to work to keep it. In 1599 she asked [godson] John Harington's wife how she kept her husband's affection: the wife replied that it was by her own love and obedience, which persuaded him of her affection which he then reciprocated. Elizabeth confided that 'after such sort do I keep the goodwill of all my husbands, my good people, for if they did not rest assured of some special love toward them, they would not readily yield me such good obedience'. Elizabeth had deliberately chosen the role of a loving queen, and she played it throughout her reign—but it was only a role.

During her reign, Elizabeth enjoyed political power while maintaining the devotion of the English people.

Queen Elizabeth projected an image of herself as a loving virgin mother, devoted to the interests of her children, whose love was warmly reciprocated. It was an image which, after some early difficulties, seems to have been widely accepted: the English came to believe what they had been told. It was the virgin part of the image which proved most difficult to put over: partly because of general assumptions about the natural relationship of the sexes, and partly because of the Queen's own conduct, it was for some years generally assumed that she was Dudley's mistress. In 1560 and 1561 there were widespread rumours, from Essex across to Devon, that the Queen was pregnant by Robert Dudley [the earl of Leicester], and when Dudley's wife was found dead there were persistent stories around London and the Midlands that he had poisoned her with Elizabeth's connivance. The Spanish ambassador reported the popular outrage at what was thought to be the Queen's disgraceful misconduct: 'The cry is that they do not want any more women rulers, and this woman may find herself and her favourite in prison any morning'. The attempt to do a deal with Philip II in 1561 also leaked out, and seemed to show that Elizabeth and Dudley would sacrifice the Gospel to their own fleshly lusts. In the London area at least, Dudley took most of the blame, but the rumours did the Queen's own reputation no good and suggested that she was no more than the pawn of her paramour. . . .

Devotion to the Queen

The emotional loyalty which individuals felt towards the Queen could be very intense. In 1585 a Sussex lawyer wrote on the flyleaf of the family Bible:

> I heartily pray the Almighty God to send a long, prosperous and happy life and reign to our good Queen Elizabeth and send us all grace that we may all live in his fear as good and dutiful subjects to our said gracious sovereign lady and queen, and all die before the sorrowful days of England shall come if God take her from us before the end of the world. And for that if for our sins he shorten her days, as he did the days of good King Edward, and yet he will grant me the grace to die at her feet before her, and that at the end of all things which is at hand we may joyfully rise again to life everlasting with perpetual joy and felicity. Amen! Amen!

In 1589 a bored Westminster schoolboy doodled over his text of

Julius Caesar: the name 'Elizabeth' is everywhere, and in a margin the couplet

> The rose is red, the leaves are green,
> God save Elizabeth, our noble queen.

The mingling of patriotic and religious sentiments had become common, and, as in the case of the Sussex lawyer, devotion to God, devotion to England, and devotion to the Queen necessarily went together. This was a product of the highly influential image of the Queen as a Protestant heroine, the saviour of English religion, and defender of the Gospel. This was not an image created officially for the Queen, but one thrust upon her by her Protestant subjects. From the beginning of the reign the Protestants had presented Elizabeth as their queen, in the hope that she would grow into the role. At her accession, ballads and pageants portrayed her as 'Deborah, judge and restorer of the house of Israel', and in 1563 John Foxe's *Acts and Monuments* told how she had been protected by God through the bloody reign of her sister so that she could restore true religion. Especially in the dangerous 1580s, Elizabeth was seen as the Protestant bulwark against Catholic plotting in England and Catholic armies in Europe: more than twenty Protestant books were dedicated to the Queen in that decade, many of them volumes of anti-Catholic polemic.

But the problem with the 'Protestant heroine' image was that Elizabeth did not always live up to it. London Protestants were horrified in 1561 when they heard of the plan to get Spanish support for a Dudley marriage by offering concessions on religion, and it took Elizabeth almost a decade to re-establish her Protestant credentials. Fortunately for her, the northern revolt of 1569 and the papal bull of excommunication made her again the darling of the Protestants. There was another public relations crisis in 1579, when the mask of the Protestant heroine slipped once more: there was a public outcry when it seemed that Elizabeth would marry [François, duke of] Alençon, and the future of the Protestant religion again seemed in doubt. It is probably true that the popular agitation was master-minded by Leicester and his political allies, but there was plenty of support for it. John Stubbs's *The discovery of a gaping gulf* was so dangerous precisely because it showed that Elizabeth was not conforming to her

Protestant image, and implied that she would lose the devotion of her Protestant subjects unless she did so. It was only partly an excuse when Elizabeth blamed her people for her refusal to marry Alençon: when it came to the crunch she had to play the Protestant role, even though she had not chosen it. She dared not shatter the image created for her.

Elizabeth had trouble when she did not live up to her unofficial image as the Protestant heroine—and she also had trouble when she was unable to live up to her official image as loving mother of her children. This was certainly true in the 1590s, when war, heavy taxation, harvest failure, and trade disruption combined to create economic crisis. The claim that Elizabeth ruled in the interests of all her subjects, and was the protectress of the poor, began to ring hollow, and her government was abused. In 1591 an Essex labourer was saying that the people should pray for a king, for 'the queen is but a woman, and ruled by noblemen, and the noblemen and gentlemen are all one, and the gentlemen and farmers will hold together so that the poor can get nothing'—'we shall never have a merry world while the queen liveth'. In the following year, another Essex labourer was saying that 'this is no good government which we now live under, and it was merry England when there was better government, and if the queen die there will be a change'.

It was argued in both Essex and Kent that Philip II would be a more solicitous ruler than Elizabeth, and that a Spanish invasion might be no bad thing. Even among non-Catholics, the reign of Mary was coming to seem like a golden age. In Middlesex, too, there was criticism of Elizabeth: in 1591 a yeoman 'desired and wished her dead', and in 1592 two sailors were complaining loudly against her rule. In 1602, when a constable warned a yeoman to obey the Queen's laws, he was told, 'Why dost thou tell me of the queen? A turd for the queen!' In Staffordshire, county officers had difficulty in collecting wartime taxes, and there was contempt for the Queen and her laws. It is significant that scandalous stories about the Queen's sexual relationships surfaced again. In 1591 an Essex couple were saying that Elizabeth had had several children, but that Leicester had stuffed each of them up the palace chimney and burned them alive. In Dorset in 1598, Edward Francis chimed that Elizabeth had three children by noblemen, and England would have been better if she had been murdered twenty years before so the country could have been ruled by a king.

In her last years, Elizabeth was losing the devotion of her subjects. There was, at best, an amused tolerance of the old woman's doings, with few signs of real affection. There was criticism of the celebration of her Accession Day, as it became increasingly difficult to see 17 November 1558 as the inauguration of a new age of peace and plenty. As early as 1583 Archbishop Whitgift had to justify the festival in a sermon, and in 1601 Thomas Holland published a defence of the celebrations against charges of idolatry. Elizabeth's earliest biographers, [William] Camden and [John Harold] Clapham, both testify to the mounting chorus of criticism of her rule from both nobles and people, and the French ambassador thought 'the English would never again submit to the rule of a woman'. Attendance at Court declined, and Elizabeth was much angered by her aristocracy's neglect. The Queen no longer held the undivided loyalty of her subjects, who had found new—and male—heroes.

Religious Observances of an Elizabethan Lady

Lady Margaret Hoby

Information about the private lives of Elizabethan women is scarce. For the most part, the few diaries and letters that do exist do not discuss private matters. Lady Margaret Hoby, a pious Protestant member of the Yorkshire gentry, used her diary, excerpted here, as a record of her daily religious observances, including prayer, meditation, reading, and at least one daily visit to church. In addition to an account of her spiritual life, Lady Hoby recorded routine domestic events. She began her diary in August 1599 and continued until July 1605. The following excerpts reveal the religious and domestic life of a devout woman living through the final years of the Elizabethan Age.

Munday 13 [August 1559]

In the Morninge after priuat praiers and order taken for diner, I wrett some notes in my testament tell :10: a clock : then I went to walk, and, after I retourned home, I praied priuatly, read a chapter of the bible, and wrought[1] tell dinner time : after I walked a whill with Mr Rhodes[2] and Then I wrought, and did som things about the house tell :4: then I wrett out the sarmon into my book preached the day before, and, when I had again gone about in the house and giuen order for supper and other thinges, I retourned to examination and praier : then I walked tell supper time, and, after Catichisinge,[3] medetated awhill of that I had hard, with mourninge to god for pardon both of my omition and Commition wherin I found my selfe guilte, I went to bed. . . .

---

1. *wrought*, sewed or embroidered. Lady Hoby is engaged in needlework of some kind or another most afternoons. Usually, though not always, she is in the company of her women and listening to a reading.   2. Master Richard Rhodes, Lady Hoby's chaplain, often mentioned.   3. *Catichisinge*, the catechism became an instrument of instruction early on. The most influential catechism was prepared by Alexander Nowell and printed in an authorized edition in 1570. This was the one used most extensively in private religious instruction.

Lady Margaret Hoby, *The Private Life of an Elizabethan Lady: The Diary of Lady Margaret Hoby, 1599–1605*, edited by Joanna Moody. Gloucestershire, England: Sutton Publishing, 1998.

Saterday 18

After I was readie I praied priuatly, and, because I was weak and had paine in my head, I wret litle but wound yearne and walked tell dinner time : after which I went about the house, and did walke abroad, workinge litle all that day because of my weaknes, least I should be disabled to keepe the Lordes day as I desired and am bound : before supper, I praied and examened my selfe, not so perteculerly as I ought to have don, which I beseech the Lord to pardon for his christs sack, and giue me grace here after to be more carefull : then I walked tell supper time : after supper I taked wth Mr Rhodes of the lordes praier, and, after lector, I medetated a litle of that I had hard, and so to bed.

The Lordes day 19

After I was redie I betooke me priuat praier: then, because Mr Hoby was not well, I kept him Kompanie tell the sarmon time, and did eate my breakfast : that done, I thank god who gaue him will and abelitie, we went to church, where we receiued the sacrementes : after I came home I praied and so to dinner, att which, and after, both my selfe did talk and heare of more worldly mattres then, by godes assistance, I will here after willingly doe : tell :3: a Clock I was with Mr Hoby, not so Care full, the Lord forgiue it me, as I ought, to medetate of what I hard, speakinge and thinking of many Idle mattres : then we went to Church and, after the sarmon, I walked tell 6: a clock, about which time I praied and examened my self, crauing pardon for these my infirmites : after, I went to supper : after which, tell praier time, I walked and, after repeticion[4] went to bed: . . .

Teusday 21

after 1 was readie I praied, and then I went awhile about the house and so to breakfast, and then to work, tell coueringe came : then I went to priuat praier but was interrupted : after I had dined I went to work tell 6:, and walked a little abroad, and then Came to examenation and praier: after, I walked a litle, and so

---

4. *repeticion*, probably the repetition of psalms or the day's epistles, sermons and teaching. Sermons were important for they furnished both entertainment and intellectual exercise. Children and servants were catechized about the preacher's utterances and notetaking was usual. Lady Hoby kept a sermon book for future reference.

to supper : after which I went to praiers, and, Nut long after, ac-
cordinge to my wonted vse, to bed, saue only I did not so deli-
gently think of that I had hard, which I beseech the Lord to pardon, for Christ sack Amen Amen . . .

Thursday 23

In the morninge I praied : then I took order for thinges about the
house tell I went to breakfast, and sonne after I took my Coach[5]
and went to Linton wher, after I had salluted my mother, I
praied, and then, walkinge a litle and readinge of the bible in my
Chamber went to supper : after which I hard the Lector and
sonne after that went to bed

Friday 24

In the morninge, beinge readie, I praied, then brak my fast with
Mr Hoby, and so reed[6] to church : after the sarmon I presently
went to dinner, after which I passed the time in talk with some
freinds, and then went to priuat praier : that don I took the aire
in the Coach with Mr Hoby, and so cam in and walked in the
garden, medetatinge of the pointes of the sarmon and prainge
tell hard before I went to supper : and after supper went to pub-
lect praier and thence to bed: . . .

September 1599, 1 *Saterday*

After praier in the morninge, I, beinge not well, did heare Mr
Rhodes read of Gyffard vpon the songe of Sallemon:[7] sone after
I went to breakfast, and so walked allmost tell dinner time : then
I Came in, and praied, and so to dinner : after which I walked
about the house, barne, and feeldes, and, when I Came home, I
praied priuat with Mr Rhodes, wherin I had more comfort then
euer I receiued in my Life before, I praise god : then I went to
take my Beesse, and, after that, I returned to priuat praier my

5. The covered carriage, or coach, was becoming very popular in London and the sur-
rounding countryside by the end of the sixteenth century. The fact that Lady Hoby had
a coach of her own in Yorkshire is evidence of her pragmatism, sense of fashion, and
wealth.   6. *reed*, rode, but can be 'read'. In Yorkshire dialect ee can become the dipthong
ee—a, giving two separate syllables. Lady Hoby often writes 'reead' for 'read'.   7. George
Gifford (d. 1620), Puritan divine and well-known preacher, deposed for nonconformity,
1584. He published theological works, including *Sermons vppon the Songe of Salomon* (1598).
The book to which Lady Hoby refers was dedicated to the Earl of Essex, her brother-in-
law by her first marriage.

selfe and examenation : then I went to se my Honnie[8] ordered, and so to supper : after which I went to lector, and soone after to bed: . . .

Tewsday beinge Christes day: 25:[9]
After priuat praier I reed of the bible, eate my breakfast, and went to Church: then I Com home and praied: after dinner, I went a while about the house, then I Caused one to Read vnto me and, beinge not well, I did omitte my orderarie exercise of praier tell after supper : then I hard repetition and praers and, after I had talked a whill to Litle purposse, I went to examenation and priuat praers, and so to bed: . . .

The 23 *of March* [1603]
Mr Hoby receiued Letters w[ch] Came from the preuie Counsill to the Lord presedent and all the Iustesis of peace, that our Quene was sicke, w[ch] wrought great sorow and dread in all good subiectes hartes: these Letters were dated the :16: of March

March: 1603: *The:* 26:
this day, beinge the Lordes day, was the death of the Quene published, our now kinge Iames of Scotland proclaimd kinge to succeede hir : god semd him along and Hapie Raing, amen. . . .

Aprill: 11:
This day Mr Hoby and my selfe tooke our Iournie from Hacknes,[10] and that night lay at Linton, wher I entertained my Cos-

8. *Honnie*, honey was particularly important for culinary use and preserving fruit. In about 1600 it was discovered that fruit could be preserved in sugar, but some time before jam was made with it. Lady Hoby may also have made honey ale, generally known as mead. Books could give advice, eg: Sir Hugh Pratt, *A Closet for Ladies and Gentlewomen, or, the Art of Preserving, Conserving and Candying* (1608, and 6 edns to 1636). Lady Hoby must have performed tasks such as this at the same time each year but she does not routinely mention them.   9. Christmas Day. Lady Hoby noted on 22 that she was making preparations, but there is no mention here of rejoining, nor evidence of festivity in the 14 days till Epiphany. She spends the evening talking 'to Litle purpose', which could imply intolerance of whatever Christmas celebration was allowed to take place in the Hackness household. Maybe there was some leniency for the less zealous. Puritans did not like merriment at this time, on the grounds that it was a heathen festival. In 1644 they would forbid celebration along with religious services by Act of Parliament and order it to be kept as a fast. In the Yorkshire dialect Christmas is Kersmass or Kessamas. The traditional festival pie, which could be enormous, consisted of an elaborately decorated crust containing an assortment of goose, chicken, pigeon and partridge with spices.   10. The Hobys are going to London for the funeral of the Queen.

sine Dakins wiues daughter to serue me: the day followinge we all went to Yorke

The: 12:

the :13: day Mr Hoby and I, wth our owne Companie, went to Dankester : the :14: day to Newarke: the :15: to stilton: the 16: to ware: ;and the 17: to london, wch was the Lordes day, and gott thether in time to Mr Egertons exercises

---

Tribute to Lady Margaret Hoby

Lady Margaret Hoby lived another twenty-six years after her last diary en-try, but nothing is known of her in those remaining years. She died at the age of sixty-three. On September 6, 1633, her body was laid to rest in St. Peter's Church, Hackness. Sir Thomas Hoby erected a decorative black mar-ble tablet in memory of his wife. The inscription on the monument inside the altar rails (still in place) indicates that Lady Hoby never faltered in her spiritual life or good deeds.

The Lady Margaret Hoby, late wife of Sr Thomas Posthvmvs Hoby Knight, and sole Davghter and heire of Arthvre Dakins Esqr by Thomasin his wife, after she had lived seven and thirty yeares and one moneth wth her said hvsband in mvtvall entire affection to both their extraordinary comfortes, and had finished the woork that God had sent her into this world to performe, and after she had attained vnto the begining of the sixty third year of her age, on the fovrth day of the seventh moneth of that yeare, it was the will of Almighty God to call her fovrth of this vale of miserie; and her body was bvryed in this chancell, on the sixt day of the same moneth (beinge September An° 1633) soe neer vnto the bodies of her sayde father and of her sayde mother (wch was interred by her sayde fathers bodie on the thirteenth day of November An° 1613) as that all three will become but one heape of dvste. Whilst this lady remained in this naturall life, she helde a constant religious covrse in performing the dvties reqvired of every faithfvl Child of God, both in their pvblike and private callings: not only by propagetinge his holy word in all places where she had power, but alsoe by exercisinge her selfe dayly in all other particvler christien dvties, and endevoures to performe the whole will of God through her faithe in Christ.

Quoted in *The Private Life of an Elizabethan Lady: The Diary of Lady Margaret Hoby, 1599–1605,* ed. Joanna Moody. Gloucestershire, England: Sutton Publishing, 1998.

The: 18: *day*
all our men and Horsses rested, and the next day we sent them
downe into the Contrie

The 28: *day:*
Was our Late gracious Quene buried at wesminster [Westmini-
ster Abbey], in that sort as became so great a prince. . . .

June 7: this day
this day Mr Hoby and my selfe remoued from London into kent,[11]
to Mr Bettnames house, wher, I praise god, I had my health very
well

The 12: *day* [October]
the most of this day was spent in the church : and at night I, after supper, I praied publickly and priuatly, and went to bed

The: 13: *day:*
After praier I did eate, went about my beuse, & after diner I talked
w[t] Mr Rhodes: then went to praier and, sonne after, to supper. . . .

The 23 *day*
this day I hard the plauge was so great at whitbie that those w[ch]
were cleare shutt themselues vp, and the infected that escaped
did goe abroad : Likewise it was reported that, at London, the
number was taken of the Liuinge and not of the deed: Lord
graunt that these Iudgmentes may Cause England w[t] speed to
tourne to the Lord[12]

11. The Hobys move out of London after the King's order on 29 May that all should
leave on account of the plague and not return until the coronation. James was crowned
on 25 July at Westminster.   12. This gives an indication of how the plague was regarded
as a punishment from God.

Weddings and Social Pageantry

Richard L. Greaves

Richard L. Greaves was born in Glendale, California, in 1938. He earned his doctorate at the University of London. Greaves taught at several colleges and universities before moving to his current position as a specialist in early modern British history at Florida State University in Tallahassee. He has written and edited twenty-five books, including numerous volumes dealing with religious and social views and practices in Elizabethan England. In the following excerpt taken from *Society and Religion in Elizabethan England*, the author explores the regulations, traditional customs, and the social pageantry of weddings.

Weddings were one of three great social spectacles used by the monied and landed classes to reinforce social order through pageantry. Weddings, christenings, and funerals reflected status in the divinely ordained hierarchy. For some, other ceremonies focused, for example, on court, the legal and academic institutions, or the investiture of ecclesiastical dignitaries, but weddings, christenings, and funerals lacked such exclusiveness. It was natural therefore that some Elizabethans imitated their betters by engaging in pageantry not befitting their social status. Such activities prompted complaints, like that of William Burton, the Puritan vicar of St. Giles, Reading, that it was not appropriate for "euery obscure Gentleman" to solemnize a marriage with the sound of trumpets, as if he were a prince or person of high calling.

[Reformer Heinrich] Bullinger's handbook on marriage prescribed a simple Protestant service. Once the contract was made he thought a wedding should not be deferred excessively. The social customs of the engagement banquet and laying the engaged couple together were unsuitable. Weddings must be performed in churches, with prayer and a sermon. Bullinger expected rela-

---

tives and neighbors to proceed to the service soberly and discreetly, in comely apparel and without pomp or drumming and piping. After the wedding he approved a simple dinner, but sumptuous banquets and wasted food were not tolerated. Social responsibility should be manifested through gifts to the poor. Customary wedding dances, with the "lyftinge vp and discoueringe of the damesels clothes and of other wemens apparell," were denounced. In effect, Bullinger wanted a simpler celebration of weddings; writing largely for a bourgeois audience in an essentially republican state, he showed no interest in weddings as pageantry to reinforce social order.

The church regulated the weddings and some of the accompanying social rites. The prescribed form for solemnizing matrimony in the *Book of Common Prayer* manifested continuity with the ancient Sarum [modified Roman] rite. There were some changes, including replacement of the mass by a sermon, but the married couple was still required to partake of the Eucharist. Protestant reformers preferred that the wedding take place in the church proper, but the older custom of performing the ceremony at the church door or on the church porch never died out during Elizabeth's reign. . . .

Wedding Regulations

To prohibit such abuses the Church of England imposed regulations, beginning with one requiring a couple to recite the catechism prior to marriage. A second regulation stipulated that banns must be published three times on Sundays or holy days before a wedding. The bishops sought to enforce this injunction in visitations, and [Bishop John] Whitgift inquired in 1577 if ministers in the diocese of Worcester were improperly asking banns twice in one day. It was possible to wed without banns by procuring an ecclesiastical license, but this was more expensive. . . .

A third regulation to control marriages required that a wedding be performed in the parish church of one or both persons being married. In visitation articles and injunctions the bishops tried to enforce this, and the canons of 1597 and 1603 curtailed licensing abuses. Licenses were issued to Anglicans and Puritans alike. In the diocese of York there were five licenses in 1590, six in 1591, fifteen in 1592, and seventeen in 1597. Metropolitan injunctions required churchwardens and sworn-men to present to the ordinary twice each year the names of those who married outside their parish churches or without banns. Yet throughout the age, the gentry and nobility preferred to be married in private chapels rather than parish churches, especially in the north. Sometimes there were legitimate reasons for this. The dowager Lady Elizabeth Russell, Sir Robert Cecil's aunt, wanted her son married in her house at Blackfriars, London, in 1596, preferring a private occasion with a few friends rather than a magnificent affair. Sometimes a private home was more appropriate for second marriages. . . .

A fourth regulation controlled the times of weddings. Although the church preserved medieval prohibitions on inappropriate times, such rules were not included in the canons or *Book of Common Prayer*, though the bishops reiterated them in visitation articles. No marriages were to take place from Advent Sunday until eight days after Epiphany, from Septuagesima Sunday until eight days after Easter, and from the Sunday prior to Ascension Day until eight days after Pentecost. John Terry explained: "The purpose of the church of Christ, in forbidding Marriages about the times of the three great solemnities of Christians was, lest by the more free vse of these earthly pleasures and delightes which abound most commonly at marriage feastes, the peoples mindes should bee somewhat hindered from the carefull preparation to receaue the holy sacrament." Puritans and Separatists regarded such prohibitions as superstitious, but most Elizabethans avoided these periods, particularly Lent. April and November were popular wedding months, falling after the Easter season and before the beginning of Advent. Clergy who violated the prohibitions were subject to ecclesiastical punishment. During the accepted periods, weddings were preferably to be held during daylight hours, since marriage was judged a work of light. . . .

The Wedding Ceremony

Any simplification of weddings tended to reduce their influence as pageants reflective of the social order. Such pageantry was important enough to prompt resistance to simplification, though some instances of plainer ceremonies are due to the application of religious principles. Weddings of the peerage were traditionally gala affairs. . . .

In a 1586 wedding at the home of Anthony Browne, Viscount Montagu, the number of nobility and gentry present was so great "as it was thought there were not ten gentlemen of Sussex, which might dispend two hundred pounds lands [*sic*] by yeare, that were absent." At the wedding supper, approximately 1,500 were served; "the beere tap neuer left running, during the space of foure daies; a time wherein a great part of the good prouision was spent, to the founders praise and the feeders releefe.". . .

Gentry weddings tended to be scaled down versions of their noble counterparts. That between Edmund Cooke, a Kentish gentleman, and Elizabeth, daughter of the London gentleman John Nicolls, in July 1562, reflected peers' ceremonies and included anti-Catholic amusement. The ceremony featured a sermon by [Thomas] Becon and was attended by the lord mayor and aldermen of London. Dinner followed at the Bridgehouse, the afternoon was taken up with music and dancing, and after a late supper a midnight masque was performed. . . .

In London, the merchant community emulated the weddings of the landed classes. . . . It is hardly surprising that merchants emulated the landed aristocracy, in view of the intermarriages. Blurring the visual symbols of social hierarchy perhaps enhanced the prestige of the merchants and planted seeds of resentment in some landed aristocrats.

Evidence is scarcer for wedding ceremonies of other groups. Yeomen celebrated with a wedding dinner at the bride's house, sometimes with both families sharing expenses. Guests might be required to give donations for their drinks, hence the term "bridale." A classic example of wedding pageantry as a reinforcement of the social hierarchy appears in a 1563 marriage covenant for the children of two Yorkshire yeoman families. The bride's father was required to provide her "with all maner of wedding apparel, as shall be seemly and comely for his and her calling.". . .

Wedding Celebrations

Weddings were social occasions of merriment and often community fellowship. In a village, it was a social duty to invite neighbors to weddings as well as christenings, funerals, sheep-shearings, and harvest celebrations. Not to do so might incite retribution, particularly if the offended person were a witch. Celebrations had a way of getting out of hand, as the groom's friends might commence feasting and drinking before the wedding and continue afterwards for perhaps as long as ten days. The celebrations were often filled with profane songs, dancing, games (often involving kissing), outdoor sports, and, for the well-to-do, masques. . . .

Weddings were not only social pageants intended to reflect and reinforce the social order, but also community gatherings replete with feasts, games, music, and dancing. Whereas clerics tended to be amenable to the former, the abuses of the latter caused concern, and presumably reinforced the desire of reformers for simpler celebrations. Yet too much movement in this direction would have weakened the wedding as a buttress (through its pageantry) of the social hierarchy. . . .

Pageantry in weddings enhanced the maintenance of the traditional order. Aristocratic weddings, whether Anglican or Puritan, were often gala affairs that reflected social rank and provided ostentatious hospitality. Some Puritans reacted against the pageantry, preferring simpler celebrations. This quest for simplicity, as well as a dislike of popish relics, was behind the hostility of more radical Puritans and the Separatists toward wedding rings. Separatists advocated civil marriage, which Anglicans and Puritans found unacceptable. The established church sought to maintain control over weddings by restricting their times and places, requiring banns, and insisting on recitation of the catechism by the prospective bride and groom. Further regulations were enforced by ecclesiastical and civil authorities to control the drinking and rowdiness that often accompanied lower-class weddings, which were occasions for community fellowship. To the extent that religious differences over wedding services were expressed, they involved the Separatists and more radical Puritans with their objections to traditional rites accepted by Anglicans and moderate Puritans. On the whole, however, in the areas of parental consent, weddings, and widowhood and remarriage, there was broad agreement among Anglican and Puritan writers, though their record of success in persuading the laity to follow their ideals was checkered.

Educational Practices

A.H. Dodd

Elizabethan England had no national system of public educa-tion; however, the importance of education for the social, cul-tural, and economic strength of the country was recognized. Schooling varied according to gender, location, and wealth with literacy highest among the upper class and in the cities. A.H. Dodd, author of the following reading, was born in Wrexham, Wales, in 1891. He taught in the history department at Bangor University from 1919 to 1958. His published works include books on Elizabethan England and histories of Wales. In this excerpt from *Elizabethan England*, Dodd presents an authoritative and vivid picture of educational practices in Elizabethan England.

The child, it has been said, was in Elizabethan eyes just a diminutive and exceptionally troublesome adult; it was not heaven that lay about us in our infancy. Nor was there much idea of progression, whether in the individual or the community: no one had yet coined the blessed word 'evolution'. The general be-lief was rather in cycles of life succeeding each other, as it were spirally, each repeating the experience of the last at a different level. The history of the race is not that of an advancing army, but of an army marching and counter-marching against an enemy, now captive, now freed again: for long weary years Satan is loosed on the world, then for just as long he is in chains. Individ-ual life is not a steady development but a sequence of short life-times, each with its rhythm of growth and decay: the seven-year climacteric, or Shakespeare's seven ages—excepting the first, which is barely on the human plane, and the last, which repeats it. Degree, the essential basis of society, did not mean a gradation of stepping stones from class to class for the enterprising and wor-thy, but a series of layers, each a miniature but self-contained so-ciety, with escape to the next layer always a possibility, but not an ambition to be encouraged. Even Elizabethan repasts, as we have seen, were a succession of courses, each a balanced meal in itself!

Stages of Education

So too in education. Elizabethans did not think as we do in terms of an educational ladder; rather each stage of education repeated in a more complex form the content of the last. The lad learning his catechism is introduced to the same circle of ideas as the divinity student at Oxford, with the ifs and buts left out; the university curriculum repeats the grammar school curriculum, but amplifies it; the delinquent student is subject to the same discipline of docked rations, impositions and flogging as the schoolboy; the married man not yet graduated from the parental roof is still under parental discipline with his younger brothers. It is in keeping with all this that the painters of the age should so often portray children and new-born babes as complete but tiny adults, or Shakespeare assure us that the child is father to the man. Perhaps the branch of education of which this is least true is the one to which least attention was devoted in the age of Elizabeth: primary education. So far as it existed, and we really know very little about it in detail, it was not a diluted version of grammar school education but rather an acquisition of the mechanical equipment (reading and writing) without which there could be no formal education at all. . . .

Naturally this business of learning one's letters was often carried out at home, under care of the mother or, in grander households, the tutor or domestic chaplain: he might well be able to go further than this and prepare his charges for the university. The widespread practice among the gentry of sending their sons and sometimes their daughters to board in other gentle households meant that the tutor might have under his charge a miniature private school, especially if he had gained a wider reputation: was not this how in Italy many of the Renaissance academies sprang up? And of course here the pupil would learn much that was not taught in the grammar school: a modern language, perhaps, like French or Italian. . . .

None of this met the case of the labourer, artisan or husbandman who did not aspire to the grammar school for his children but did want them to read the Bible for themselves instead of depending on the verbal instruction of the priest: perhaps to go further and learn to write and cast accounts. How far these mild ambitions could be achieved depended very much on local conditions. In some parishes there were endowments, administered by the churchwardens, under which the parson could add a few pounds to his meagre stipend by keeping school; a very energetic and conscientious incumbent might do it voluntarily. After all it was an obligation on him, laid down in royal injunctions and often emphasised in episcopal visitations, to provide an exhibition at university or grammar school for one lad of promise out of every £100 he earned, and how else could such promise be discovered in parishes where there was no endowed school? On the other hand, how many livings with actual cure of souls brought in as much as £100? So a good deal of this elementary instruction was given in small and ephemeral schools of the type of the Victorian dame school, kept perhaps by the sexton or bell-ringer at a mark a year, or by 'poor women or others whose necessities compel them to undertake it as a mere shelter from beggary'.

There is every indication that schools of this type were widespread even in remote shires, and that many of them went well beyond the rudiments; but only by chance did they leave any record of themselves. A census taken of the poor of Norwich in 1571, extending down to six-year-olds, revealed a surprising number who at seven or eight were attending school. . . .

Schools Affected by Religious Turmoil

Schools, like everything else, suffered from the religious upheavals of the early part of the century. The former cathedral schools soon recovered; those attached to great monasteries like Canterbury and Westminster were refounded by a better distribution of their old endowments. Smaller monastic foundations did not fare so well, but some of them struggled to their feet again with the help of private or municipal benefactions; a lot of these schools had in fact been very small affairs with little educational influence outside their own community. The heaviest casualties were among the chantry schools that taught grammar: some were refounded by local generosity; many vanished for ever. The Speaker of the House of Commons at the opening of the reign reckoned that the country was poorer than it had been by a hundred grammar schools.

The 'lay' foundations of the fourteenth and fifteenth centuries, from Winchester and Eton down to country grammar schools founded by trade gilds or by private citizens or squires, suffered only the temporary set-backs caused by the frequent 'purges' of masters and scholars during successive phases of the Reformation; for of course no school was completely free of clerical jurisdiction. An article which was a hardy annual among the instructions to the bishops and among their enquiries at visitations, was the condition and number of grammar schools in their dioceses—'a matter of no small moment, and chiefly to be looked into by every bishop in his diocese', as the council put it in a letter to Archbishop Grindal in 1580. Here crown and bishops, gentry and merchants were at one. The reestablishment of a sound educational system was at once a guarantee of the religious settlement and the social order (the equivalent indeed of propaganda in the modern state), a contribution towards the economic health and therefore the political independence of the state in these years of stress, and a means of maintaining both the social dignity and the practical competence of the rising generation of gentry. In these circumstances the leeway was soon made up. It has been reckoned that before the end of the reign, through the munificence of merchants, churchmen, gentlemen, even yeomen (the nobility to a less marked degree), England had as many schools as ever. . . .

Universities suffered even more heavily than schools from the troubles of the Reformation; obviously it was harder in such conspicuous institutions to escape the watchful eye of the bishop or his commissary. Purges and counter-purges had wrought havoc in the ranks of fellows and scholars and left deep gashes in chapels and in libraries, where books of the wrong theological colour had often been consigned to the flames. Naturally parents were frightened of sending their young to encounter these risks. 'Universities do wondrously decay already' [Bishop Hugh] Latimer had assured the boy-king [Edward VI], and again, 'It would pity a man's heart to hear that that I hear of the state of Cambridge; what it is in Oxford, I cannot tell'. We can: it was worse, in proportion as the old scholastic theology had been more firmly entrenched there. Once the Elizabethan settlement had given promise of stability, however, both universities soon made up the lost ground and forged still farther ahead. . . .

The Curriculum

The curriculum, in school and college alike, was still formally based on the scheme inherited from the educational practice of the Roman Empire: the *trivium* of grammar, logic and rhetoric and the *quadrivium* of arithmetic, geometry, astronomy and music. Grammar of course meant Latin grammar, the key to all other studies since it was the medium of instruction and the international language of learning. Greek, although it had now been taught for two or three generations, still had something of the status of a newcomer, not universally welcomed. But in other respects the New Learning and the Reformation between them were bringing about many readjustments in the traditional scheme of things. Probably the most important was the printed word: lectures need no longer be literally 'readings' now that the student could read his texts for himself, often in editions from his own university press. A growing sensitiveness to style added importance to rhetoric: Latin was still a flexible living language, and an imaginative teacher could use his teaching of it both to develop literary taste and to stimulate current interests. On the other hand, the close association of logic with theology in the medieval scheme called for a new approach, often a stormy one, to this branch of the *trivium*, and the enthronement of the English Bible as the *vade mecum* of divinity brought in a new text book. Even mathematics had had important theological bearings, and in consequence shared in the general shift of emphasis; for a time it lost much of its academic status, in school and university alike, and developed rather as a 'practical' subject or a private hobby, outside the normal curriculum. The practical needs were chiefly those of the business man and the navigator; as a hobby it was pursued by the numerous dabblers in astrology. In both aspects the redoubtable Dr. [John] Dee, the queen's Welsh astrologer, counted for more than academic lectures. Robert Recorde, a fellow-Welshman who taught at both universities, introduced outside readers to the Arabic sciences of algebra and arithmetic, in text books which had an enormous vogue for a century and more after his death in 1558.

Astronomy suffered with mathematics; the telescope lay in the future, and what was taught was an antiquated survival unaffected by the new theories of Copernicus. It is characteristic that Sir John Davies's fine poem *Orchestra*, published in 1596, describes the universe on orthodox medieval lines and dismisses the Copernican system in an aside. . . .

Modern subjects fared little better. We have seen something of the provision for modern languages in private schools or by private tuition. Ancient history you read in your Latin or Greek authors; for modern history you depended on the chronicles which were to be found in every gentleman's library. Similarly with geography: apart from the outdated stuff included in astronomy, it could be picked up from the many books of travel issuing from the press. . . .

The universal Cinderella of studies was the mother tongue. Voices had already been raised, weighty ones too, in favour of English both as a medium of instruction and as a subject worthy of study in itself, but so far educational practice had not responded. English grammar was learned through Latin grammar, English style through translation from Latin, literary criticism through rhetoric. The results were not unimpressive. Much worse was the case of the Welsh pupil, who had no printed Welsh classics to draw on. The language had to be transmitted orally at home, with the aid of a few recently printed primers, grammars and dictionaries; what saved it from extinction, and with it a rich body of inherited culture, was the Welsh Bible. . . .

Elizabethan View of Education

To the Elizabethan mind education was neither a public service provided by the state nor a marketable commodity, though commercial habits of mind were giving fuller play to this second aspect; it was rather a work of charity like alms-houses and hospitals. Ideally, if Christians all did their duty after their means, school and college were within reach of all, financially and geographically. They very nearly were for all willing and able to profit by them. . . . Girls often went to school at the primary stage, but after that they had to depend on home tuition. The quality of that must have been pretty high, judging by results: upper-class women of the age could have shown a clean pair of heels educationally to any later generation until we reach the opening of the universities to women, and even the squire's or farmer's wife could often write a decent letter. The age of Shakespeare had little to blush for in its educational practice.

A Child's Garden of Sprites: English Renaissance Fairy Poetry

Warren W. Wooden

Warren W. Wooden, former professor of English at Marshall University in Huntington, West Virginia, died in 1983 at the age of forty-two. At the time of his death, the highly acclaimed Renaissance scholar was researching the origins of children's literature in England from 1500 to 1700—the first comprehensive treatment of children's literature during this period. The selection below was excerpted from *Children's Literature of the English Renaissance*. In this essay delivered at the Modern Language Association (December 1980), Wooden examines fairy poetry as a vehicle for social commentary. He also explains why fairy poetry was popular in the English Renaissance as well as the psychological implications of children's fascination with fairyland.

Although the Elizabethan era, defined broadly as encompassing both the late sixteenth and early seventeenth centuries, has been aptly designated the "Golden Age" of English fairy poetry, it is well to recall that the poets of the period neither invented the fairies nor originated fairy poetry. As scholars and folklorists remind us, the fairies themselves have a rich history which extends in one direction back to the classical pantheons of Greece and Rome and in another deep into the roots of folk beliefs among the Celtic and Teutonic peoples who settled Great Britain. And at various intervals, these creatures found their way into literature, into [John] Gower and [Geoffrey] Chaucer and the "literary" tradition as well as the anonymous charms, ballads, and lyrics of the popular tradition. But only in the Elizabethan era did fairy poetry fire the imagination of the finest poets and appeal to a broad audience eager for news of the world of Faery. Setting aside Lord Berners' translation of *Huon of Bordeaux* (1534) which introduced Oberon to the English public, Edmund Spenser in his *Faerie Queene* (1590) first popularized fairies during the period with his accounts of the stirring deeds of elphine knights and ladies in a romantic fairyland inhabited by magicians, fays, monsters, and spirits of all sorts. Then in the mid-1590s, William Shakespeare utilized fairies as a major plot constituent of *A Midsummer Night's Dream* (performed c. 1595; printed 1600), transforming their traditional portrayal (one enthusiastic scholar even asserts Shakespeare "created a new supernaturalism" in his presentation of the fairies) and making them accessible to a wider and more representative audience. Shakespeare's portrayal of tiny creatures borne on gossamer wings proved so immediately popular that his conception became *the* literary image of fairies, inaugurating a flood of unabashedly imitative fairy poetry. . . .

Clearly the ambiance, social and intellectual, of the late sixteenth century in England was a major factor in the literary exploitation of the fairies. Perhaps the decline in the belief in fairy magic and its role in the terrors of the night (a decline of belief which contrasts oddly with the new emphasis on rooting out witchcraft which King James brought to England) made of them fit ornaments for poetry. Or perhaps, as [Minor W.] Latham suggests, the new yeoman class of poets, men like Shakespeare and [Michael] Drayton, brought with them the folklore of the villages and, in appealing to the burgeoning class of first-generation literates, turned to the familiar elves of the countryside for their supernatural machinery. In this regard, the great wave of English nationalism that marked the 1590s may also have been a contributing factor to the literary popularity of such indigenous sprites as Robin Goodfellow, alias Puck, who, like Queen Elizabeth herself, was "mere English." In any event, Shakespeare's assay into fairy poetry in *A Midsummer Night's Dream* demonstrated convincingly how ripe were the times for the fairy folk. Perhaps also the dynamic mix, sometimes almost a tension, of belief and disbelief in fairy magic stimulated the poets of the age, with credence widespread in the countryside though declining in the cities. . . .

Fascination with Fairies

Speculation on the audiences of fairy poetry invariably leads to a discussion of the child as reader, since fairy stories and poems constitute a branch of literature children have always appropriated as their own. The key point to stress here is that in the Renaissance the choice is the child's rather than the author or bookseller's. With the exception of some schoolbooks, grammars, catechisms, and the like, children were not singled out for attention by the book trade as a special audience. Instead, Renaissance children were automatically part of the literary marketplace through such works as Aesop's *Fables*, a perennial favorite of all ages. Those authors, such as Shakespeare and Drayton, who sought a broad and representative public for their poetry thus wrote for a dual audience of adults and children. Therefore, there is little to be gained by seeking a special type of literature for entertainment targeted to the pre-adult population during our period; it does not exist. Yet children read, often voraciously, in the literature of the day, and for that reason a broad definition of a children's book, such as that promulgated by Sheila Egoff, is applicable: "In the true sense, a children's book is simply one in which a child finds pleasure." Thus children read and thrilled to works such as John Foxe's great *Book of Martyrs* (1563), accessible in churches and public places all over England, which, in its combination of minute descriptions of hair-raising tortures with popular piety, the whole illustrated with graphic woodcuts of various tortures, could hardly have failed to rivet the attention of any but the most squeamish child. But children's preferred choice of reading matter was doubtless verse, for, as one modern critic has observed, "poetry, unlike other forms of literature, is common ground for both children and grown-ups."

The fairies and their lore, done up into attractive verse and accompanied by an occasional woodcut, exerted a particular appeal to children which not even Foxe's horrific stories could rival. The adult world fed children's natural fascination with the magical and mysterious by positing a special connection between children and fairies centered upon the fairies' most notorious activity, the exchange of fairy offspring for human children. "The thing that everyone knows about the fairies," explains K.M. Briggs, "is that they covet human children and steal them whenever they can. No account of fairies is complete without the mention of this practice." The timid child could experience a half-pleasurable thrill at the prospect of being kidnapped by marauding fairies, while the more adventurous youth could indulge secret dreams of actually being a changeling, possessor of fairy powers unknown and untapped, reservoirs of mystery and potency foreign to both adults and peers. Certainly children who were slightly built, dark-featured, or, most commonly, simply mischievous, must have been familiar enough with humorous adult exclamations about changelings to have set them reflecting on the fairies. . . .

The changeling swaps were but one of a host of fascinating fairy activities familiar in the folklore of the countryside and the villages. Children learned of their tricks, of the domestic rituals through which the fairies might be propitiated, and of the habits

Shakespeare used fairy poetry, which gained popularity during the English Renaissance, in his play A Midsummer Night's Dream *(pictured).*

and character of Robin Goodfellow or Puck, the most famous country spirit, from oral traditions and tales before they began to read. Puck, especially, was a familiar spirit to children and likely a convenient one also since all manner of domestic mischances and accidents might be blamed on him, for he was, as M.W. Latham notes, "the national practical joker" during our period. And the fairy lore of the countryside (England was still predominantly rural country in the Renaissance) received concrete reinforcement from the fairy hills and dancing rings which dotted the countryside. A child could hardly escape the fairy presence, even should one wish to resist their allure. And a knowledge of the fairies and their ways could be a positive boon to a child, for the fairies were great gift-givers and he who was in the fairies' favor was fortunate indeed. Stories of fabulous fairy treasure buried in hills or left in bundles in the fields, by wells or pools, or the other places frequented by the creatures are legion. Meanwhile, the child who respected the fairies' regard for cleanliness and neatness and did his chores faithfully was often rewarded in the morning by a fairy gift of a six-pence in his shoes. In sum, the lore of the fairy world impinged at numerous points upon childhood and the folk tales of the tricks and doings of the fairies were an essential part of childhood during the English Renaissance.

Children thus imbibed a good deal of knowledge about fairies from their culture, including specifics about fairy activities which particularly involved children. Other causes for children's fascination with fairies may be adduced, such as their apparently instinctive affinity for the miniature, as in children's particular concern for puppies, kittens, birds, and the like. But it is most tempting to move beyond the social reference of this fairy lore to speculate upon the psychological attraction the world of fairy must have held for the Renaissance child. The fairies formed an invisible empire headquartered, according to popular opinion, underground inside the hills and caverns of the English countryside. They had a king and queen who presided over a state with laws and rules which not only fairies but mortals transgressed at their peril. The fairies thus constituted a kingdom within a kingdom, with alternate rules and life-styles altogether independent of the regulations and restrictions of the adult world familiar to children.

In fact, the fairy world, exalting mischief and the marvellous, often mocks the rules and values of the human adult world, with the characteristic activities of the fairies a burlesque of rational adult behavior. Against an adult world which constantly exhorted children, in church, school, and home, to grow up and adopt adult standards and values as rapidly as possible, the pastoral fairy world of escape and release stands as a striking antithesis, a realm of caprice and inversion, a subversive paradigm which must have delighted any child with spirit. And although diminutive in size, unlike real children the fairies were very potent through their possession of magical powers, enabling them to command propitiatory rites (the bowl of cream left on the doorstep overnight is one of the most familiar) from the adult population. As William Empson has observed in another context, "children like to think of being so small that they could hide from grown-ups and so big that they could control them." In the fairies of Shakespeare and his followers, children have an alter ego which combines freedom from adult supervision with magical potency. And the fairies' occasional guerrilla raids on the adult model of ordered civilization make of them a literary rallying point for those such as pre-adults disenfranchised by their society.

Before leaving the rich topic of the psychological implications of children's fascination with fairyland, one final point of identification between the world of fairy and the psyche of the Renaissance child may be mentioned: the conception of time. As pastoral dwellers, probably descendents of agricultural deities as the folklorists suggest, the fairies are responsive to the round of the seasons, but neither to larger nor to more particular time frames. The fairies appear to lead a kind of timeless existence, living for the day, oblivious to the years, bound only by the seasonal cycle. The similarity of this time-consciousness to that characteristic of childhood is striking, adults are bewildered by both. The stories of adults who inadvertently or rashly blunder into a fairy ring or one of the entrances of the fairies' underground kingdom and return after what they believe to be a brief sojourn, of hours or days, to find themselves years older illustrate this point. (Folklorists even trace the Rip Van Winkle story back to a fairy archetype of this nature.) From the stock of Renaissance fairy beliefs, then, there seems ample evidence to support the theory that the attraction of children for this body of folklore, and its literary embodiment, works on several different levels, including a psychological appeal to a sense of revolt, mischief, and freedom from adult supervision and restraint. . . .

Fairy Culture

Fairies are country spirits, alien to the city and to many urban values, and they enter the city rarely and with reluctance; usually, to traffic with the fairies, one must go to the countryside, their domain. When they do pay these infrequent visits, as at Midsummer or Halloween, to exchange a child or bless a favorite mortal, mischief and confusion often attend them, even when their intent, as in *A Midsummer Night's Dream*, is good. This seems to be the case because the fairies represent an ethic foreign to that of daylight urban society (theirs is "the night rule" as Puck calls it) and when the two collide, confusion is an inevitable consequence. Although the appeal of the fairy ethic to an audience of children has been discussed, it is also necessary to notice the formal function of the fairy ethic, especially as it resembles the model of the traditional literary pastoral. [C.L.] Barber notes many of the obvious pastoral trappings of Shakespeare's fairies, but he does not press the functional similarity between the fairy ethic and activity and that of the literary pastoral. The pastoral in the Renaissance presents an alternate life-style in contrast to urban existence, and it is inherently a criticism of urban values. Fairyland often borrows the trappings of pastoral not only on its surface but in its function; it too amuses and instructs to life by proposing an alternate lifestyle and value system by which quotidian existence may be measured, judged, and, ideally, improved. Of course, the fairy frolic, like the sedentary shepherd's life in the literary pastoral, is not intended as a literal or practicable alternative to maturity and civilization; neither is ideal. Like the pastoral and the state of childhood itself, however, fairyland manifests customs, values, and behavior alien to adult urban culture, and yet all these variant life-styles, whatever the manner of their metaphoric presentation, can teach important lessons about the values of play, release, harmony, and the natural life. And like the pastoral, the fairy culture of the countryside affords a detached vantage point for studying adult civilization where, as Puck truly sees, "Lord, what fools these mortals be.". . .

Decline of Fairy Poetry

The contrast between fairy ways and human ones, explicit in Shakespeare and [Ben] Jonson and clearly implicit in Drayton, disappears by the time of [Robert] Herrick, the Dutchess of New-castle, and the later seventeenth-century fairy poets. Minifica-tion, one technique in the presentation of Shakespeare's fairies, becomes a self-sufficient end in itself and the pastoral sphere of fairy activity becomes increasingly isolated, until fairyland ceases to have any real relevance or relationship to the world of human beings. Fairy poetry becomes static, tedious, and irrelevant. Thus, as [Floris] Delattre laments, fairy poetry "may be said to be extinct in England about 1650."

The poets' loss of interest in the fairies as a vehicle for psy-chological release, social commentary, or poetic significance is at least as important to the death of fairy poetry in the seventeenth century as the putative general decline of belief in the fairy world. . . . Nevertheless, the post-Renaissance construction in the scope, aims, and target audience of English fairy poetry should not be allowed to obscure the achievement of the Elizabethan laureates of the little folk. In their poetry, adults no less than chil-dren could find delight and release in an imaginative fairy world which retained its relevance to the human world.

A Foreigner's Impressions of Elizabethan England

Paul Hentzner

Many foreigners, chiefly Germans, visited England during the reign of Queen Elizabeth. In 1598, lawyer Paul Hentzner, a native of Brandenburg, Germany, toured England. Hentzner was the tutor of one of his traveling companions, Christoph Rehdiger, a young nobleman of Silesia. Most of the time, the party journeyed on horseback. Hentzner recorded his observations in a journal, which he published in 1612. In the extract below, Hentzner describes the sights of England as well as his impressions of Elizabethan society.

Elizabeth, the reigning Queen of England, was born at the Royal Palace of Greenwich, and here she generally resides, particularly in summer, for the delightfulness of its situation. We were admitted by an order, which Mr. Rogers (Daniel Rogerius) had procured from the Lord Chamberlain, into the Presence-Chamber hung with rich tapestry, and the floor, after the English fashion, strewed with hay, through which the Queen commonly passes in her way to chapel. At the door stood a gentleman dressed in velvet, with a gold chain, whose office was to introduce to the Queen any person of distinction that came to wait on her. It was Sunday [Sept. 6, N.S.], when there is usually the greatest attendance of nobility. In the same hall were the Archbishop of Canterbury, the Bishop of London, a great number of Counsellors of State, Officers of the Crown, and Gentlemen, who waited the Queen's coming out, which she did from her own apartment when it was time to go to prayers, attended in the following manner:—

First went Gentlemen, Barons, Earls, Knights of the Garter, all

Paul Hentzner, "Extracts from Paul Hentzner's Travels in England, 1598," *England as Seen by Foreigners in the Days of Elizabeth and James the First*, edited by William Brenchley Rye. New York: Benjamin Blom, Inc., 1967.

richly dressed and bareheaded; next came the Lord High Chancellor of England, bearing the seals in a red silk purse, between two, one of whom carried the royal sceptre, the other the sword of state in a red scabbard, studded with golden fleur-de-lis, the point upwards; next came the Queen, in the 65th year of her age (as we were told), very majestic; her face oblong, fair but wrinkled; her eyes small, yet black and pleasant; her nose a little hooked, her lips narrow, and her teeth black, (a defect the English seem subject to, from their too great use of sugar); she had in her ears two pearls with very rich drops; her hair was of an auburn colour, but false . . . upon her head she had a small crown, reported to be made of some of the gold of the celebrated Luneburg table; her bosom was uncovered, as all the English ladies have it till they marry; and she had on a necklace of exceeding fine jewels; her hands were slender, her fingers rather long, and her stature neither tall nor low, her air was stately, her manner of speaking mild and obliging. That day she was dressed in white silk, bordered with pearls of the size of beans, and over it a mantle of black silk shot with silver threads; her train was very long, the end of it borne by a marchioness; instead of a chain, she had an oblong collar of gold and jewels. As she went along in all this state and magnificence, she spoke very graciously, first to one, then to another (whether foreign ministers, or those who attend for different reasons), in English, French, and Italian; for besides being well skilled in Greek, Latin, and the languages I have mentioned, she is mistress of Spanish, Scotch, and Dutch. . . . Whoever speaks to her, it is kneeling; now and then she raises some with her hand. While we were there, William Slawata, a Bohemian baron, had letters to present to her; and she, after pulling off her glove, gave him her right hand to kiss, sparkling with rings and jewels—a mark of particular favour. Wherever she turned her face as she was going along, everybody fell down on their knees. The ladies of the court followed next to her, very handsome and well-shaped, and for the most part dressed in white. She was guarded on each side by the gentlemen pensioners, fifty in number, with gilt halberds. In the antechapel, next the hall where we were, petitions were presented to her, and she received them most graciously, which occasioned the acclamation of *God save the Quene Elizabeth!* She answered it with *I thancke you myn good peupel.* In the chapel was excellent music; as soon as it and the service were over, which scarcely exceeded half-an-hour, the Queen returned in the same state and order, and prepared to go to dinner. But while she was still at prayers, we saw her table set out with the following solemnity:—

Dinner Ritual

A gentleman entered the room bearing a rod, and along with him another who had a table-cloth, which after they had both knelt three times, with the utmost veneration, he spread upon the table, and after kneeling again, they both retired. Then came two others, one with the rod again, the other with a salt-cellar, a plate and bread; when they had knelt as the others had done, and placed what was brought upon the table, they too retired with the same ceremonies performed by the first. At last came an unmarried lady of extraordinary beauty (we were told that she was a countess) and along with her a married one, bearing a tasting-knife; the former was dressed in white silk, who, when she had prostrated herself three times, in the most graceful manner approached the table and rubbed the plates with bread and salt with as much awe as if the Queen had been present. When they had waited there a little while, the yeomen of the guard entered, bareheaded, clothed in scarlet, with a golden rose upon their backs, bringing in at each turn a course of twenty-four dishes, served in silver most of it gilt; these dishes were received by a gentleman in the same order as they were brought and placed upon the table, while the lady-taster gave to each of the guard a mouthful to eat of the particular dish he had brought, for fear of any poison. During the time that this guard, which consists of the tallest and stoutest men that can be found in all England, 100 in number, being carefully selected for this service, were bringing dinner, twelve trumpets and two kettle-drums made the hall ring for half-an-hour together. At the end of all this ceremonial, a number of unmarried ladies appeared, who with particular solemnity lifted the meat off the table, and conveyed it into the Queen's inner and more private chamber, where after she had chosen for herself, the rest goes to the ladies of the Court. The Queen dines and sups alone with very few attendants; and it is very seldom that any body, foreigner or native, is admitted at that time, and then only at the intercession of some distinguished personage.

The Queen's Park

Near this palace is the Queen's park, stocked with various wild animals. Such parks are common throughout England, belonging to those that are distinguished either for their rank or riches. In the middle of this is an old square tower, called *Mirefleur*, supposed to be that mentioned in the Romance of Amadis de Gaula; and joining to it a plain, where knights and other gentlemen use to meet at set times and holidays to exercise on horseback.

It is worthy of observation, that every year upon St. Bartholomew's Day, when the Fair is held, it is usual for the Mayor, attended by the twelve principal Aldermen, to walk into a neighbouring field, dressed in his scarlet gown, and about his neck a golden chain, to which is hung a Golden Fleece, and besides, that particular ornament [the collar of SS], which distinguishes the most noble Order of the Garter. During the year of his magistracy, he is obliged to live so magnificently that foreigner or native, without any expense, is free, if he can find a chair empty, to dine at his table, where there is always the greatest plenty. When the Mayor goes out of the precincts of the City, a sceptre, a sword, and a cap are borne before him, and he is followed by the principal Aldermen in scarlet gowns, with gold chains; himself and they on horseback. Upon their arrival at a place appointed for that purpose, where a tent is pitched, the mob begin to wrestle before them, two at a time; the conquerors receive rewards from the Mayor. After this is over, a parcel of live rabbits are turned loose among the crowd, which boys chase with great noise. While we were at this show, one of our company, Tobias Salander, Doctor of Physic, had his pocket picked of his purse, with nine crowns . . . which without doubt was so cleverly taken from him by an Englishman who always kept very close to him, that the Doctor did not in the least perceive it. . . .

Impressions of England

The soil is fruitful and abounds with cattle, which inclines the inhabitants rather to feeding than ploughing, so that near a third part of the land is left uncultivated for grazing. The climate is most temperate at all times, and the air never heavy, consequently maladies are scarcer, and less physic is used there than anywhere else. There are but few rivers. Though the soil is productive, it bears no wine; but that want is supplied from abroad by the best kinds, as of Orleans, Gascon, Rhenish, and Spanish. The general drink is ale, which is prepared from barley, and is excellently well tasted, but strong and intoxicating. . . . There are many hills without one tree or any spring, which produce a very short and tender grass, and supply plenty of food to sheep; upon these wander numerous flocks extremely white, and whether from the temperature of the air or goodness of the earth, bearing softer and finer fleeces than those of any other country. This is the true Golden Fleece, in which consist the chief riches of the inhabitants, great sums of money being brought into the island by merchants, chiefly for that article of trade. The dogs here are particularly good. It has mines of gold, silver and tin (of which all manner of table utensils are made, in brightness equal to silver, and used all over Europe), of lead, and of iron, but not much of the latter. The horses are small but swift. Glass-houses are in plenty here.

English Customs

The English are grave like the Germans, lovers of show; followed wherever they go by whole troops of servants, who wear their masters' arms in silver fastened to their left arms, and are not undeservedly ridiculed for wearing tails hanging down their backs. They excel in dancing and music, for they are active and lively, though of a thicker make than the French; they cut their hair close on the middle of the head, letting it grow on either side; they are good sailors and better pirates, cunning, treacherous, and thievish; above 300 are said to be hanged annually at London; beheading with them is less infamous than hanging; they give the wall as the place of honour; hawking is the common sport with the gentry. They are more polite in eating than the French, consuming less bread but more meat, which they roast in perfection; they put a great deal of sugar in their drink; their beds are covered with tapestry, even those of farmers; they are often molested with the scurvy, said to have first crept into England with the Norman Conquest; their houses are commonly of two stories, except in London, where they are of three and four, though but seldom of four; they are built of wood, those of the richer sort with bricks, their roofs are low, and where the owner has money, covered with lead. They are powerful in the field, successful against their enemies, impatient of anything like slavery; vastly fond of great noises that fill the ear, such as the firing of cannon, drums, and the ringing of bells, so that in London it is common for a number of them that have got a glass in their heads [are drunk] . . . to go up into some belfry, and ring the bells for hours together, for the sake of exercise. If they see a foreigner very well made, or particularly handsome, they will say, "It is a pity he is not an Englishman". . . .

September 14th. As we were returning to our inn [at Windsor], we happened to meet some country people celebrating their Harvest-home . . . their last load of corn they crown with flowers, having besides an image richly dressed, by which perhaps they would signify Ceres; this they keep moving about, while men and women, men and maidservants, riding through the streets in the cart, shout as loud as they can till they arrive at the barn. The farmers here do not bind up their corn in sheaves, as they do with us, but directly they have reaped or mowed it, put it into carts and convey it into their barns.

There is a certain sect in England called Puritans. These, according to the doctrine of the Church of Geneva, reject all ceremonies anciently held, and admit of neither organs nor epitaphs in their places of worship, and entirely abhor all difference of rank among ecclesiastics, such as bishops, abbots, &c. They were first named Puritans by the Jesuit Sanders. They do not live separate, but mix with those of the Church of England in the colleges.

Departure

We came to Canterbury on foot. Being tired, we refreshed ourselves with a mouthful of bread and some ale, and immediately mounted post-horses, and arrived about two or three hours after nightfall at Dover. In our way to it, which was rough and dangerous enough, the following accident happened to us. Our guide or postillion . . . a youth, was before with two of our company, about the distance of a musket-shot, we by not following quick enough had lost sight of our friends; we came afterwards to where the road divided, on the right it was down hill and marshy, on the left was a small hill; whilst we stopped here in doubt, and consulted which of the roads we should take, we saw all on a sudden on our right-hand some horsemen, their stature, dress, and horses exactly resembling those of our friends; glad of having found them again, we determined to set on after them; but it happened through God's mercy, that though we called to them, they did not answer us, but kept on down the marshy road, at such a rate that their horses' feet struck fire at every stroke, which made us with reason begin to suspect that they were robbers, having had warning of such, or rather that they were nocturnal spectres, which as we were afterwards told, are frequently seen in those places; there were likewise a great many Jack-w'-a-lanthorns . . . so that we were quite seized with horror and amazement. But fortunately for us, our guide soon after sounded his horn, and we following the noise, turned down the left-hand road, and arrived safe to our companions; who, when we had asked them if they had not seen the horsemen who had gone by us? answered, not a soul. Our opinions, according to custom, were various upon this matter; but whatever the thing was, we were without doubt in imminent danger, from which that we escaped the glory is to be ascribed to God alone.

We take ship for Calais (Sept. 24). In our company were the noble Lord Wilhelm Slawata, a Bohemian baron, with his servant Corfutius Rudth, a noble Dane, Wilhelm and Adolphus ab Eynatten, brothers, from Juliers, and Henricus Hoen their relation. Before we set sail from hence [*i.e.* Dover], each of us was obliged to give his name, the reason of his visit to England, and the place to which he was going. This having been done, and permission to depart obtained, our valises . . . and trunks were opened by those who are appointed for this object, and most diligently examined for the sake of discovering English money, for no one is allowed to carry out of England more than ten English pounds. Whatever surplus there may be, it is taken away and paid into the royal Exchequer.

Arts, Entertainment, and Leisure Pursuits

CHAPTER
3

Chapter Preface

In Elizabethan England, laws were enacted to regulate sports and entertainment. Certain laws banned commoners from participating in activities that were considered sports by the upper classes. For example, ordinary people were forbidden by law to hunt deer. If a poor man killed a deer to feed his starving children, he faced death by hanging. This was to protect the activity as a sport for the nobility.

Sports that prepared the poor to participate in battle, on the other hand, were encouraged by the government. Although laborers were forbidden to take part in sports during the week, on Sundays archery practice for the working class was mandatory, just as it had been for two hundred years.

Other laws, such as the Act of 1512 that had made games such as tennis, bowls, and skittles illegal, were meant to deter the poor and middle class from playing games rather than being productive members of society. Laws were passed that made it illegal for any artisan, laborer, husbandman, or serving man to play the banned games. These laws did not apply to the nobility, however. Many noblemen had tennis courts and bowling alleys attached to their houses.

People of all classes including royalty delighted in attending extremely brutal sports such as bull and bear baitings. Placing bets on the results of these violent sports was common. Oddly, the same legislators who passed statutes forbidding lower classes to play bowls or tennis allowed these blood sports. Historian M. St. Clare Byrne wrote: "The average Elizabethan was not sensitive to the spectacle of physical suffering, either in human beings or in animals." Illustrative of this statement is the fact that great crowds gathered to watch torturous deaths, such as beheadings, hangings, or burnings, as a form of entertainment.

Despite government regulations, the Elizabethan found ways to relieve the tedium of long work hours. He played as hard as he worked. With gusto and enthusiasm, Elizabethans participated in the available sports and pastimes of the age.

Music and Society

John Buxton

John Buxton was born in Cheshire, England. He was a lecturer in English literature at Oxford University. His publications include, in addition to numerous contributions to newspapers and journals, volumes of verse and books in the field of English studies. *Elizabethan Taste*, from which this reading is excerpted, the first study of its kind, provides an in-depth understanding of Elizabethan culture. Buxton examines the response of the Elizabethans to the music composed for them.

Of all the arts music is the least confined by national boundaries. In the time of Queen Elizabeth the English language, which has since . . . become the language of most of the New World, was restricted to a small population on an island far removed from the Mediterranean origins of the Renaissance, and scarcely any Italian or Spaniard or Frenchman would have deigned to learn it. Most would have thought . . . that English was a barbarous tongue unsuited to poetry, and it was not until the eighteenth century that English began to be recognized abroad as one of the chief literary languages of the world.

But the English achievement in music, sacred and secular, vocal and instrumental, was immediately saluted on the Continent. . . .

While the Italians and the French supposed that English poetry could not exist, they knew that English music might equal or surpass their own.

This was no new discovery. In the first half of the fifteenth century English musicians, of whom the greatest was John Dunstable, had had much influence on the Flemish composers, and the theorist of that school, Joannes de Tinctoris, regarded England as the principal source of the art of music. Martin le Franc, about 1440, also paid tribute to Dunstable and his English contemporaries. The two English universities instituted degrees in music in the fifteenth century, long before any Continental uni-

John Buxton, *Elizabethan Taste*. New York: St. Martin's Press, 1963. Copyright © 1963 by John Buxton. Reproduced by permission.

versity, which was proof of an early interest in music as a serious branch of learning; and most of the Elizabethan composers were proud to describe themselves on their title-pages as Bachelor or Doctor of Music.

Queen Elizabeth, like her father Henry VIII and her sister Mary, was herself an accomplished musician. [Thomas] Tallis and [William] Byrd, in dedicating to her in 1575 their *Cantiones Sacrae*, praised her for the elegance of her voice and the dexterity of her fingers. Richard Mulcaster in some Latin elegiacs in praise of their music which he contributed to the book paid a compliment to the Queen which, however confidently it was to be expected, need not therefore be discounted:

> The Queen, the glory of our age and isle
> With royal favour bids this science smile;
> Nor hears she only others' labour'd lays,
> But, artist-like, herself both sings and plays.

In her youth she 'composed ballets and music, and played and danced them' but she also kept up with the new fashions in music, would sing ayres and accompany her singing on the lute; and she played the virginals [a small spinet]. . . .

The Queen's Musicians

The Queen was proud to have at least sixty musicians in her service. These included both the singers of the Chapel Royal and the instrumentalists of the Queen's Musick. Various lists of the musicians, and of the instruments which they played, survive, from which it is possible to follow certain changes of fashion during the Queen's reign. In 1558 she had forty-one musicians of whom half were foreigners, most of these North Italians from Venice, Cremona, Milan, and elsewhere, and among them were five members of the Bassano family which provided many musicians in the royal service from 1538 to the time of the Civil War. . . .

Musicians would play for the Queen's private pleasure, or would provide music at the tournament or at masques. Elizabethan masques were simple compared with the extravagant shows staged by Inigo Jones in the time of King James and King Charles, and the music required was also much simpler. At the masque written by Philip Sidney for the Queen's visit to Wanstead in 1578, the only music was of recorders and cornets; but for the masque [Thomas] Campion wrote for Lord Hay's wedding in 1607, which was presented before the King in Whitehall, he used almost the whole of the resources of the King's Musick. Campion arranged the musicians with great care in several groups: 'on the right hand were consorted ten musicians, with bass and mean lutes, a bandora, a double sackbut, and an harpsichord, with two treble violins; on the other side . . . were placed nine violins and three lutes; and to answer both the consorts (as it were in a triangle) six cornets and six chapel voices were seated almost right against them, in a place higher in respect of the piercing sound of those instruments'.

The Chapel Royal

The chapel voices would be from the Chapel Royal, a much more important institution, which had been in existence at least as early as 1135, and to which the tradition of English music owed much of its splendour. In the fifteenth century Joannes de Tinctoris had observed that the greatest encouragement to the art of music in England came from the Chapel Royal, and this continued to be so throughout the sixteenth and early seventeenth centuries, when among the gentlemen of the Chapel Royal were such distinguished musicians as Tallis, [Christopher] Tye, [William] Mundy, [William] Byrd, [Thomas] Morley, [John] Bull, [Thomas] Tomkins, and Orlando Gibbons. The Chapel Royal was an institution, not a building, and its members would accompany the Queen on progress, as they accompanied her father to the Field of the Cloth of Gold, as they would accompany King James to Scotland and King Charles to Canterbury when he went to welcome his Queen. By the time Queen Elizabeth came to the throne it had thirty-two members, of whom twelve were boys. The post of organist was not established until Thomas Tallis's day: previously various gentlemen must have been expected to act as occasion served. The position of Gentleman of the Chapel Royal carried much prestige: it was worthy of mention on a title-page together with a degree from either university. The gentlemen were quite well paid, and had the advantage of being in daily contact with the Court, with all the possibilities of aristocratic patronage which this gave them. . . .

The Queen's example must have encouraged her courtiers towards accomplishment in music—to be 'skilful auditors'—and to the patronage of musicians: both accepted as necessary to the ideal of the complete man. Scholarly scepticism of recent years has a little damaged the older picture of the Renaissance gentleman being able to sing a part at sight, or to accompany a song of his own on the lute; but perhaps it is time to effect some restoration. Morley's famous dialogue, where Philomathes is put to shame for his inability to sing his part, is discounted: Morley's enthusiasm is supposed to have run away with him. But Morley was saying very much what [composer] Thomas Whythorne had observed in Italy forty years before: 'I perceived that among such as were of any account, they were esteemed to be but rudely and basely brought up who had no knowledge in music, or at the least able to play or sound on some musical instrument or else to sing pricksong [music written with dots]. . . .

Children and Music

It is obvious that some provision was made for teaching the children of the house to play or sing at all early age. Often the task would be given to one or other of the servants: Sir William Petre gave his housekeeper, Mary Percy, extra money for teaching his daughters to play the virginals; the Kytsons of Hengrave Hall employed a man named Cosen to teach their children the virginals; in 1558 the Earl of Rutland paid a lutenist named Weston ten shillings for teaching his page to play on the lute. In 1586 Roger Manners wrote to the then Earl of Rutland to assure him that his daughter's music was not being neglected: 'I have not forgotten the Lady Elizabeth, but have a servant to play the virginals with her when Symons is away'. Symons, presumably, was her regular teacher and in the Earl's employ; probably the Earl had taken him with him to London. A year later Edward Paston was writing to the Earl to recommend an organist from Norwich to teach his daughter the virginals. Thomas Bancs, who taught singing to Sir William Cavendish's children, was not included among the servants receiving wages and livery: probably he was employed solely as a music master. Music was written specially for teaching: so Richard Alison framed some of the compositions in *An Hour's Recreation in Music* 'with two trebles, necessary for such as teach in private families'. Thus the teacher might be a servant or might be a professional musician brought into the household for a time, as Thomas Whythorne was variously employed in the household of the Earl of Warwick and of other but unidentifiable people. Most fortunate of all these aristocratic children was the daughter of the Earl of Northumberland whose tutor in 1579 was none other than William Byrd.

Inevitably some of these children would, through lack of aptitude, abandon the attempt to play or sing when they grew up; but the general respect for musical accomplishment, and the expectation that a person of any account would be able to play and sing, must have ensured that the majority kept up their music. . . .

A family tradition of music of this kind, rather than the presence in the family of a composer of genius, can persuade us of the prestige music had in Elizabethan society, for gifts such as [composer] Michael Cavendish's occur unpredictably, but so widespread a love of music comes of deliberate choice. There was a universal acceptance of music as one of the civilized pleasures, so that anyone who aspired towards the ideal of the courtier must be able to make music in company with his friends, or for his private recreation. It was the custom, Morley says, to bring out the music books when supper was ended: he does not say, this is what I wish people would do, but, this is what most of them already do. . . .

Secular Music

The English passion for all things Italian, which led the Queen to boast that she was half Italian and Shakespeare to lay the scene of half his plays in Italy, could be even more quickly satisfied by the importation of Italian music than by the translation of Italian poetry, though for most translation would not be necessary. There was much criticism of this tardy apish nation for limping after the Italians in base imitation: Morley himself, with less justification than Shakespeare, joined the chorus of those who objected to 'the new-fangled opinions of our countrymen who will highly esteem whatsoever cometh from beyond the seas (and specially from Italy)' but he continued to publish Italian music, and to write in the Italian manner. Richard Carleton was more candid: in the preface to his *Madrigals* in 1601 he admits that he has 'laboured somewhat to imitate the Italian, they being in these days (with the most) in high request'. The composers were, after all, trying to write the kind of madrigals their countrymen wished to sing. . . .

In England the success of the popular drama delayed the appearance of true opera for half a century, till the improbable production in Commonwealth London by that incorrigible Cavalier, Sir William Davenant, of *The Siege of Rhodes*. (This production was the first in which a woman took a part on the English stage: it was such a success, in those dowdy times, that Davenant rewrote the opera with a part for a second woman.) Masques by Ben Jonson were set in *stilo recitativo* [a style of singing related to dramatic speech] as early as 1617 and 1621, by Nicholas Lanier, but these were isolated occasions, and neither *Lovers Made Men* nor *The Gypsies Metamorphosed* begot any operatic progeny. Instead of musical drama the English musicians invented the ayre, a solo song with lute accompaniment which had no Continental ancestry. The old polyphonic tradition was dying, and the assumption that unaccompanied vocal music was the proper medium for serious composers could no longer remain unquestioned. Both stringed and keyboard instruments were much improved during the sixteenth century, and indeed (Galileo's father) [composer] Vincenzo Galilei considered lutes of English workmanship better than any others. Few would yet dispute Byrd's insistence that 'there is not any music of instruments whatsoever comparable to that which is made of the voices of men'; but in saying so his own voice is raised a little, as if, for the first time, someone might be prepared to contradict. And indeed Richard Mulcaster, whose views on many things were far ahead of his time, clearly regarded learning to play an instrument as not less important than singing in the education of the young.

John Dowland's *First Book of Songs or Ayres*, published in 1597 began the series of books of lute-songs. . . .

If we look back over the history of music during the past five centuries we can see why it was that the ayre came to its sudden perfection at this time. The old dominance of unaccompanied voices would eventually give place to the dominance of the modern orchestra, of instrumental music; parallel with this great change was another, from polyphony to homophony; and though the two did not progress at the same speed, as it were, yet during the lifetime of Dowland and Campion the two revolutions reached their crises. In these great changes of taste (for that is what they were) English composers played the leading part, and in the creation of the ayre, or art-song, and in the composition of instrumental music, especially for the virginals, they did not learn from but taught the rest of Europe.

Resistance to Stage Plays

Stephen Gosson

Although bloody and lewd, Elizabethan drama expressed the exuberance and passionate intensity of the times. Playwrights responded to the demands of audiences and gave them horrific swordfights and bawdy humor. This great period of drama had many critics, mostly Puritan extremists and those who believed the plays generated much civil disorder. Stephen Gosson, author of the following excerpt, attacked the theaters and their audiences in *The School of Abuse* printed in 1579. Gosson had earlier been a poet, actor, and playwright. He later became rector of the Church of St. Botolph in Bishopsgate, London. The attacks by Gosson and other critics did little to dampen the enthusiasm for plays, however. Many writers, including dramatist Thomas Lodge and Sir Philip Sidney, offered spirited defenses of the arts against Puritan complaints.

Consider with thy selfe (gentle Reader) the olde discipline of Englande: marke what wee were before, and what we are now. . . . Cast thine eye backe to thy predecessours, and tell me howe woonderfully we have beene changed since we were schooled with these abuses. Dion saith that English men could suffer watching and labor, hunger and thirst, and beare of all storms with head and shoulders: they used slender weapons, went naked, and wer good soldiours: they fedde uppon rootes and barkes of trees: they would stande up to the chinne many dayes in marshes without victualles, and they had a kinde of sustenaunce in time of neede, of which if they hadde taken but the quantitie of a beane, or the weight of a pease, they did neither gape after meate, nor long for the cuppe a great while after. The men in valure not yeelding to Scythia; the women in courage passing the Amazons. The exercise of both was shooting and darting, running and wrestling, and trying such mais-

Stephen Gosson, *The School of Abuse Containing a Pleasant Invective Against Poets, Pipers, Players, Jesters, &c.* London: The Shakespearean Society, 1841.

teries as eyther consisted in swiftnesse of feet, agilitie of bodie, strength of armes, or martiall discipline.

But the exercise that is nowe among us is banquetting, playing, pyping, dauncing, and all suche delightes as may winne us to pleasure, or rocke us in sleepe. . . . Oh, what a wonderfull change is this! Our wrastling at armes is turned to wallowing in laddies lappes; our courage to cowardice; our cunning to riot, our bowes into bolles, and our dartes to dishes. Wee have robbed Greece to gluttony, Italy of wantonnes, Spayne of pride, France of deceite, and Duchland of quaffing. Compare London to Rome and England to Italy, you shall finde the theaters of the one, the abuses of the other, to bee rife among us. . . .

London Plays

In our assemblies at playes in London, you shall see suche heaving and shooving, suche ytching and shouldering to sytte by women; suche care for their garments that they be not trode on; suche eyes to their lappes that no chippes lighte in them; such pillowes to their backes that they take no hurte; suche masking in their eares, I know not what; suche geving them pippins to passe the time; suche playing at foote saunt without cardes; such ticking, such toying, such smiling, such winking, and such manning them home when the sportes are ended, that it is a right comedie to marke their behaviour, to watch their concreates, as the catte for the mouse, and as good as a course at the game it selfe, to dogge them a little, or follow aloofe by the printe of their feete, and so discover by slotte where the deare taketh soyle.

If this were as well noted as il seene, or as openly punished as secretely practised, I have no doubt but the cause woulde be seared to drye up the effect, and these prettie rabbets varye cunningly ferretted from their borrowes. For they that lacke customers all the weeke, either because their haunt is unknowen, or the constables and officers of their parish watch them so narrowly that they dare not queatche, to celebrate the Sabboth flocke to theaters, and there keepe a generall market of bawdrie. Not that anye filthinesse, in deede, is committed within the compasse of that ground, as was once done in Rome, but that every wanton and [his] paramour, everye man and his mistresse, every John and his Joane, every knave and his queane are there first

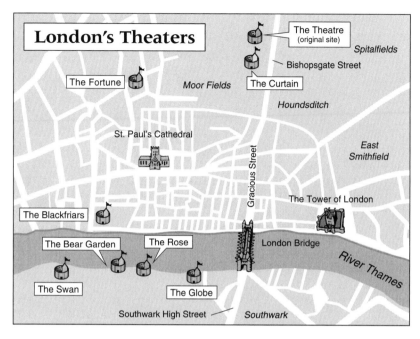

acquainted, and cheapen the marchandise in that place, which they pay for else where, as they can agree. These wormes, when they dare not nestle in the pescod at home, find refuge abrode and ar hidde in the cares of other mens corne. . . .

Perils of the Theater

I intend not to shew you al that I see, nor half that I here of these abuses, lest you judge me more wilful to teach them, then willing to forbid them. I looke stil when Players shoulde cast me their gauntlettes, and challenge a combate for entering so farre into theyr possessions, as thoughe I made them Lordes of this Misrule, or the very schoolemaisters of these abuses: though the best clarks be of that opinion, they heare not mee saye so. There are more howses then parishe churches, more maydes then Maulkin, more wayes to the wood then one, and more causes in nature then efficientes. The carpenter rayseth not his frame without tooles, nor the Divell his woorke without instruments: were not Players the meane to make these assemblies, suche multitades woulde hardly bee dawne in so narrowe a roome. They seeke not to hurte, but desire to please: they have purged their comedies of wanton speaches, yet the corne which they sell is full of cockle, and the drinke that they drawe overcharged with dregges. There is more in them then we perceive: the Divell standes at our elbowe when we see not, speaks when we heare not, strikes when we feele not, and woundeth sore when he raseth no skinne nor rentes the fleshe. In those thinges that we lest mistrust the greatest daunger doeth often lurke: the countrieman is more afraid of the serpent that is hid in the grasse, than the wilde beaste that openly feedes upon the mountaines: the mariner is more endaungered by privye shelves then knowen rockes: the souldier is sooner killed with a little bullet then a long sworde. There is more perill in close fistuloes then outward sores, in secret ambushe then mayne batteles, in undermining then playne assaulting, in friendes then foes, in civill discorde then forrayne warres. Small are the abuses, and slight are the faultes that nowe in Theaters escape the poets pen. . . .

And as some of the players are farre from abuse, so some of their playes are without rebuke, which are easily remembered, as quickly reckoned. The two prose bookes played at the Belsavage, where you shall finde never a woorde without witte, never a line without pith, never a letter placed in vaine. The Jew, and Ptolome, showne at the Bull; the one representing the greedinesse of worldly chusers, and bloody mindes of usurers; the other very lively describing howe seditious estates with their owne devises, false friendes with their owne swoords, and rebellious commons in their owne snares are overthrowne; neither with amorous gesture wounding the eye, nor with slovenly talke hurting the eares of the chast hearers. The Black Smiths Daughter, and Catilins Conspiracies, usually brought in at the Theater: the firste containing the trachery of Turks, the honourable bountye of a noble mind, the shining of vertue in distresse. . . .

These playes are good playes and sweets playes, and of all playes the best playes, and most to be liked, woorthy to be soung of the Muses, or set out with the cunning of Roscius him self, yet are they not fit for every mans dyet: neither ought they commonly to be showen. Now, if any man aske me why my selfe have penned comedyes in time past, and inveigh so egerly against them here, let him knowe that . . . I have sinned, and am sorry for my fault: he runnes far that never turnes: better late then never. I gave my selfe to that exercise in hope to thrive, but

Swiss Tourist Enjoys the Theater

Thomas Platter, a native of Basel, visited England in 1599. During his stay, he attended a performance of William Shakespeare's Julius Caesar *at the newly opened Globe as well as plays at other theaters. In his diary,* Thomas Platter's Travels in England, *the author presents a picture of the Elizabethan theater.*

On September 21st after lunch, about two o'clock, I and my party crossed the water, and there in the house with the thatched roof witnessed an excellent performance of the tragedy of the First Emperor Julius Caesar with a cast of some fifteen people; when the play was over, they danced very marvellously and gracefully together as is their wont, two dressed as men and two as women.

On another occasion not far from our inn, in the suburb at Bishopsgate, if I remember, also after lunch, I beheld a play in which they presented diverse nations and an Englishman struggling together for a maiden; he overcame them all except the German who won the girl in a tussle, and then sat down by her side, when he and his servant drank themselves tipsy, so that they were both fuddled and the servant proceeded to hurl his shoe at his master's head, whereupon they both fell asleep; meanwhile the Englishman stole into the tent and absconded with the German's prize, thus in his turn outwitting the German; in conclusion they danced very charmingly in English and Irish fashion. Thus daily at two in the afternoon, London has two, sometimes three plays running in different places, competing with each other, and those which play best obtain most spectators. The playhouses are so constructed that they play on a raised platform, so that everyone has a good view. There are different galleries and places, however, where the seating is better and more comfortable and therefore more expensive. For whoever cares to stand below only pays one English penny, but if he wishes to sit he enters by another door, and pays another penny, while if he desires to sit in the most comfortable seats which are cushioned, where he not only sees everything well, but can also be seen, then he pays yet another English penny at another door. And during the performance food and drink are carried round the audience, so that for what one cares to pay one may also have refreshment. The actors are most expensively and elaborately costumed; for it is the English usage for eminent lords or knights at their decease to bequeath and leave almost the best of their clothes to their serving men, which it is unseemly for the latter to wear, so that they offer them then for sale for a small sum to the actors.

How much time then they may merrily spend daily at the play everyone knows who has ever seen them play or act.

Quoted in G. Blackmore Evans, ed., *Elizabethan-Jacobean Drama: The Theater in Its Time.* New York: Meredith Press, 1988.

I burnt one candle to seeke another, and lost bothe my time and my travell when I had done. . . .

God hath armed every creature against his enemie: the lyon with pawes, the bull with hornes, the bore with tuskes, the vulture with tallents, harts, hindes, hares and such like with swiftnesse of feet, because they are fearefull, every one of them putting his gifte in practise; but man, which is lord of the whole earth, for whose service herbes, trees, rootes, plants, fish, foule and beasts of the fielde were first made, is farre worse then the brute beastes: for they, endewed but with sence, doe . . . seeke that which helpes them, and forsake that which hurtes them.

Man is enriched with reason and knowledge; with knowledge to serve his maker and governe himselfe; with reason to distinguish good and ill, and chose the best, neither referring the one to the glory of God, nor using the other to his owne profite. . . .

But wee, which are so brittle that we breake with every fillop, so weake that we are drawne with every thread, so light that wee are blowen away with every blast, so unsteady that we slip in every ground, neither peyse our bodyes against the winde, nor stand uppon one legge for sleeping too much, nor close upp our lippes for betraying our selves, nor use any witte to garde our owne persons, nor shewe our selves willing to shunne our owne harmes, running most greedily to those places where wee are soonest overthrowne. I can not liken our affection better then to an arrowe, which, getting libertie, with winges is carryed beyonde our reach; kepte in the quiver it is still at commandement or to a dogge; let him slippe, he is straight out of sight; holde him in the lease, hee never stirres: or to a colte; give him the bridle, he flinges about; raine him hard and you may rule him; or to a ship; hoyst the sayles, it runnes on head; let fall the ancour, all is well; or to Pandoraes boxe; lift upp the lidde, out flyes the Devil; shut it up fast, it cannot hurt us.

Let us but shut uppe our eares to poets, pipers and players; pull our feete backe from resorte to theaters, and turne away our eyes from beholding of vanitie, the greatest storme of abuse will bee overblowne, and a faire path troden to amendment of life: were not we so foolish to taste every drugge and buy every trifle, players woulde shut in their shops, and carry their trash to some other country.

Elizabethan Love Poetry

Edmund Spenser

Edmund Spenser was one of the greatest poets of the Elizabethan Age. Spenser's contemporaries considered his philosophical allegory, *The Faerie Queene*, a masterpiece. When Edmund Spenser died, poets carried his coffin to Westminster Abbey and threw into the open grave memorial elegies and the pens used to write them. The sonnets below come from his highly acclaimed work—the *Amoretti and Epithalamion* published in 1595. The poems record, in idealized form, Spenser's courtship with his future wife, Elizabeth Boyle, of Kilcoran, Ireland.

Sonnet I.

Happy, ye leaves! when as those lily hands,
Which hold my life in their dead-doing might,
Shall handle you, and hold in love's soft bands,
Like captives trembling at the victor's sight.
And happy lines! on which, with starry light,
Those lamping eyes will deign sometimes to look,
And read the sorrows of my dying spright,
Written with tears in heart's close-bleeding book.
And happy rhymes! bath'd in the sacred brook
Of Helicon, whence she derived is;
When ye behold that Angel's blessed look,
My soul's long-lacked food, my heaven's bliss;
 Leaves, lines, and rhymes, seek her to please alone,
 Whom if ye please, I care for other none!

Sonnet III.

The sovereign beauty which I do admire,
Witness the world how worthy to be praised!
The light whereof hath kindled heavenly fire
In my frail spirit, by her from baseness raised;

Edmund Spenser, "Amoretti and Epithalamion, 1595," *Elizabethan Sonnets*, vol. II, edited by Sidney Lee. New York: Cooper Square Publishers, Inc., 1964.

That, being now with her huge brightness dazed,
Base thing I can no more endure to view:
But, looking still on her, I stand amazed
At wondrous sight of so celestial hue.
So when my tongue would speak her praises due,
It stopped it with thought's astonishment;
And, when my pen would write her titles true,
It ravished it with fancy's wonderment:
    Yet in my heart I then both speak and write
    The wonder that my wit cannot endite.

Sonnet VII.

Fair eyes! the mirror of my mazed heart,
What wondrous virtue is contained in you,
The which both life and death forth from you dart,
Into the object of your mighty view?
For, when ye mildly look with lovely hue,
Then is my soul with life and love inspired:
But when ye lower, or look on me askew,
Then do I die, as one with lightning fired.
But, since that life is more than death desired,
Look ever lovely, as becomes you best;
That your bright beams, of my weak eyes admired,
May kindle living fire within my breast.
    Such life should be the honour of your light,
    Such death the sad ensample of your might.

Sonnet XVI.

One day as I unwarily did gaze
On those fair eyes, my love's immortal light;
The whiles my 'stonish'd heart stood in amaze,
Through sweet illusion of her look's delight;
I mote perceive how, in her glancing sight,
Legions of loves with little wings did fly;
Darting their deadly arrows, fiery bright,
At every rash beholder passing by.
One of those archers closely I did spy,
Aiming his arrow at my very heart:
When suddenly, with twinkle of her eye,

The Damsel broke his misintended dart.
    Had she not so done, sure I had been slain;
    Yet as it was, I hardly scap'd with pain.

Sonnet XXI.

Was it the work of nature or of art,
Which tempered so the feature of her face,
That pride and meekness, mixed by equal part,
Do both appear t'adorn her beauty's grace?
For with mild pleasance, which doth pride displace,
She to her love doth lookers' eyes allure;
And, with stern countenances, back again doth chase
Their looser looks that stir up lusts impure;
With such strange terms her eyes she doth inure,
That, with one look, she doth my life dismay;
And with another doth it straight recure;
Her smile me draws; her frown me drives away.
    Thus doth she train and teach me with her looks;
    Such art of eyes I never read in books!

Sonnet XXX.

My love is like to ice, and I to fire;
How comes it then that this her cold so great
Is not dissolv'd through my so hot desire,
But harder grows the more I her entreat?
Or how comes it that my exceeding heat
Is not delay'd by her heart-frozen cold;
But that 1 burn much more in boiling sweat,
And feel my flames augmented manifold!
What more miraculous thing may be told,
That fire, which all things melts, should harden ice;
And ice, which is congeal'd with senseless cold,
Should kindle fire by wonderful device!
    Such is the power of love in gentle mind,
    That it can alter all the course of kind.

Sonnet XL.

Mark when she smiles with amiable cheer,
And tell me whereto can ye liken it;

When on each eyelid sweetly do appear
An hundred graces as in shade to sit.
Likest it seemeth, in my simple wit,
Unto the fair sunshine in summer's day;
That, when a dreadful storm away is flit,
Through the broad world doth spread his goodly ray;
At sight whereof, each bird that sits on spray,
And every beast that to his den was fled,
Comes forth afresh out of their late dismay,
And to the light lift up their drooping head.
    So my storm-beaten heart likewise is cheered
    With that sunshine, when cloudy looks are cleared.

Sonnet LIV.

Of this world's theatre in which we stay,
My love like the spectator, idly sits;
Beholding me, that all the pageants play,
Disguising diversely my troubled wits.
Sometimes I joy when glad occasion fits,
And mask in mirth like to a comedy:
Soon after, when my joy to sorrow flits,
I wail, and make my woes a tragedy.
Yet she, beholding me with constant eye,
Delights not in my mirth, nor rues my smart:
But, when I laugh, she mocks; and, when I cry,
She laughs, and hardens evermore her heart.
    What then can move her? if nor mirth nor moan,
    She is no woman, but a senseless stone.

Sonnet LV.

So oft as I her beauty do behold,
And therewith do her cruelty compare,
I marvel of what substance was the mould,
The which her made at once so cruel fair.
Not earth; for her high thoughts more heavenly are:
Not water; for her love doth burn like fire:
Not air; for she is not so light or rare:
Not fire; for she doth freeze with faint desire.
Then needs another element inquire

Whereof she mote be made, that is, the sky.
For to the heaven her haughty looks aspire:
And eke her mind is pure immortal high.
   Then, sith to heaven ye likened are the best,
   Be like in mercy as in all the rest.

Sonnet LXXII.

Oft, when my spirit doth spread her bolder wings,
In mind to mount up to the purest sky;
It down is weighed with thought of earthly things,
And clogged with burden of mortality;
Where, when that sovereign beauty it doth spy,
Resembling heaven's glory in her light,
Drawn with sweet pleasure's bait, it back doth fly,
And unto heaven forgets her former flight.
There my frail fancy, fed with full delight,
Doth bathe in bliss, and mantleth most at ease;
Ne thinks of other heaven, but how it might
Her heart's desire with most contentment please.
   Heart need not wish none other happiness,
   But here on earth to have such heaven's bliss.

Sonnet LXXV.

One day I wrote her name upon the strand;
But came the waves, and washed it away:
Again, I wrote it with a second hand;
But came the tide, and made my pains his prey.
Vain man, said she, that dost in vain assay
A mortal thing so to immortalize;
For I myself shall like to this decay,
And eke my name be wiped out likewise.
Not so, quoth I, let baser things devise
To die in dust, but you shall live by fame:
My verse your virtues rare shall eternize,
And in the heavens write your glorious name.
   Where, when as death shall all the world subdue,
   Our love shall live, and later life renew.

Sonnet LXXIX.

Men call you fair, and you do credit it,
For that yourself ye daily such do see;
But the true fair, that is the gentle wit,
And virtuous mind, is much more praised of me:
For all the rest, however fair it be,
Shall turn to naught and lose that glorious hue;
But only that is permanent and free
From frail corruption, that doth flesh ensue.
That is true beauty: that doth argue you
To be divine, and born of heavenly seed;—
Deriv'd from that fair Spirit, from whom all true
And perfect beauty did at first proceed:
    He only fair, and what He fair hath made;
    All other fair, like flowers, untimely fade.

Sonnet LXXXVIII.

Like as the Culver, on the bared bough,
Sits mourning for the absence of her mate;
And, in her songs, sends many a wishful vow
For his return that seems to linger late:
So I alone, now left disconsolate,
Mourn to myself the absence of my love;
And, wandering here and there all desolate,
Seek with my plaints to match that mournful dove.
Ne joy of aught that under heaven doth hove
Can comfort me, but her own joyous sight:
Whose sweet aspect both God and man can move,
In her unspotted pleasance to delight.
    Dark is my day, while her fair light I miss,
    And dead my life that wants such lively bliss.

Reading Is a Popular Pastime

Elizabeth Burton

The author of the following selection, Elizabeth Burton, has written several popular histories of everyday life in England. Using official documents, letters, diaries, memoirs, and contemporary printed materials, Burton recreates the everyday life of the average citizens of the day. In the following selection excerpted from *The Pageant of Elizabethan England*, Burton describes the Elizabethans' insatiable appetite for reading materials.

Reading, to judge by the number of books and pamphlets, broadsides and ballads printed, must have been one of the major pastimes. A half-century of printing, together with far better and wider educational facilities for more people meant books to read and people to read them. The Elizabethans in fact developed a voracious appetite for reading-matter. And reading-matter was turned out in such quantity that [travel writer] Thomas Coryat remarked, gloomily, that there would soon be more books than readers.

Londoners bought books from stalls clustered round St. Paul's cathedral. Country people were served with ballads, broadsides, pamphlets, jest and riddle books by itinerant pedlars. The new, round world of the Elizabethans was what the Universe is to us. Their space travel is our known geography. Travel books were so popular that it seemed people could never have enough of them—which is how [William] Harrison came to write his book. It was intended as a part of a much larger work undertaken by Reginald Wolfe, printer to the Queen, who planned to bring out "a universall Cosmographie of the whole world, and therewith also certaine particular histories of every known nation". For the historical part he engaged Ralph Holinshed and others. But, after twenty-five years of work, Wolfe died. His backers, afraid to

Elizabeth Burton, "Of Pleasures and Pastimes," *The Pageant of Elizabethan England.* New York: Charles Scribner's Sons, 1958.

continue so vast an enterprise, decided to do only Holinshed plus a description of Britain and England. Harrison had long been working on a Chronologie of his own, so he was asked to furnish the necessary descriptions—which he did, though he says in his introduction that he "scrambled up . . . this foul frizeled Treatise".

Popularity of Travel Books

Part of the desire to read travel books arose from the fact that travel and exploration in the public imagination spelled riches.[1] Those who never travelled farther than the next village for Michaelmas fair took to voyaging and discovering treasure through books. Sir Walter Raleigh's short book with the long title—*The Discovery of the Large, Rich and Bewtiful Empire of Guiana, with a Relation of the Great, Golden City of Manoa (which the spanyards call El Dorado) and the Province of Emeria, Arromaia, Amapaia and other Countries with Rivers adioyning*—went into three editions in the year of publication (1596). Who could resist such words as Large, Rich and Bewtiful Empire, or Great Golden City or the strange poetry of Emeria, Arromaia, Amapaia?—certainly not the Elizabethans even if most of them disliked and mistrusted the author. Arrogant, they had heard he was, and he looked foreign, too, with his dark face and eyes, like a Spaniard.

An entirely different kind of sailor-author was Henry Robarts who produced pamphlet after pamphlet glorifying British seamanship and the exploits of buccaneers. Robarts, a staunch believer in patriotic propaganda even manages to attribute acts of high piracy to the providence of God. This was a very popular notion of the day. But the idea that material success, no matter how achieved, is signal proof of God's favour was neither invented by, nor did it die with, the Elizabethans.

A popular ballad of the time puts national fervour in a nutshell

You gallants all o' the British blood
Why don't you sail o' the ocean flood?
I protest you're not all worth a filbert
If once compared to Sir Humphrey Gilbert.

Yet what would the sailors have done without Richard Hakluyt?

---

1. The capital put up for Drake's voyage around the world was £5,000. The return was £600,000.

His was the greatest name of the time and his *Principal Navigations* is still one of the finest books in our language. Hakluyt, like Harrison, was a parson and, like Harrison and Robarts, was a propagandist for his country. He believed that the maritime power of England had a mission through trade and colonization, to "increase the Queen's dominions, enrich her coffers, and reduce many Pagans to the faith of Christ". Times change. Today we are reversing the process which the first Elizabethans set in motion. But it should be remembered they were as firm in their belief that it was right to initiate the process as we are that it is right to reverse it.

Interest in Science

With our own interest in science and science-fiction, it is perhaps a little surprising to find the Elizabethans no less interested in what they termed science. With few physicians available every householder felt obliged to know something of medicine. With stars so influential it would be folly not to know something of astrology and astronomy. With alchemy always on the verge of discovering the philosopher's stone it would be stupid not to keep abreast of news in this field. The, to us, almost unintelligible and seemingly endless jargon of *The Alchemist* was understood by the middle- and upper-class Englishman far better than we understand our own mushrooming scientific language.

Digests, Booklets, and Ballads

Digests, which we think of as typically modern, were also popular. John Maplet, in 1567, brought out a positively encyclopaedic digest designed for the busy and the unlearned man, under the charming title *A Greene Forest, or a Naturall Historie.* Maplet wanted to simplify university training and make it available to the ordinary man. His *Greene Forest* was a digest and homestudy course rolled into one. Divided into three sections, Animal, Vegetable and Mineral, its information was necessarily brief but what facts there were, were set out in English translated and condensed from the Latin treatises used at the universities. Maplet popularized Aristotle, Pliny, Theophrastus, Dioscorides and Cardan and brought them within reach of those who had neither Latin nor Greek; just as [poet George] Chapman, but for other reasons, "Englished" Homer. Most of the erudite works of the day were written in Latin, and it was a courtier accomplishment to translate various books from Latin into English. Elizabeth, in her later years, occupied herself in spare minutes by translating Boethius as a pastime. . . .

Then there were hundreds of booklets of popular learning of the Teach or Do-it-Yourself variety. Thomas Hill was a most prolific turner-out of such work which let tradesmen, the un-Latined and un-Greeked, into the secrets of Nature. These revelations included useful information plus a certain amount of mumbo-jumbo on gardening, astrology, astronomy, physiognomy, palmistry, botany, medicine, chemistry, bee-keeping, dream-interpretation and prediction; to say nothing of a secret recipe for turning water into wine. But the new horizons of the physical world had certainly led to new horizons of the mind, and tradesmen and apprentices could now speak with more knowledge than the clerk of the Middle Ages. . . .

Elizabethan authors on the whole were lucky; they had a public so eager to read and to learn that almost anything in print sold well—from the newly Englished masterpieces of the ancient world right down to the most ephemeral ballad.

And of ephemeral reading-matter there was no lack. Broadsides and ballads were innumerable and were, in a sense, the equivalent of our newspapers. Nearly everything could be, and was, translated into ballad form. To a nation which loved songs—even bad ones—as much as the English did, the ballad was obviously designed to be extremely popular. It did not matter how scurrilous the content nor how appalling the verse; complaints against taxes and monopolies, the purported last thoughts of executed criminals, the hatred of Pius V, the adventures of Drake and Hawkins, the competition engendered by the importation of foreign artisans, the knavery of tradesmen, the evils of wine, women and tobacco all were subjects for ballad maker and monger. The common man of the day lived in an age half-way between the Troubador and the Tabloid.

Appeal of Fiction

As for fiction, there was plenty of that. Sir Philip Sidney's *The Arcadia* was very popular in court circles as was [John] Lyly's *Eu-*

phues: The Anatomy of Wit. There was Robert Greene's *Menaphon: Camilla's Alarm to Sleeping Euphues;* and his pastoral romances such as *Pandosto: The Triumph of Time* (Shakespeare liked this so well that he borrowed the plot for *The Winter's Tale*). Greene, who called Shakespeare an "upstart crow" was a prolific writer and the big best-seller of the day. Thomas Lodge, who abandoned law for literature and literature for medicine, was popular too. . . .

On a rather less-exalted level than Sidney, Greene, and Lodge were translations from the Spanish, French, and Italian. The taste for Spanish romances, endless and inane, told with little skill and less artistry, destroys any illusions that we may have that the literary taste of the first Elizabethans was universally good. Middle-class readers were less concerned with taste than with morals (though moral excellence was certainly not always found in the original Spanish romances). Here, again, one sees a touch of the Victorian in them—or again it might be called a further example of the Englishness of the English. Yet there were realistic and low-life novels too. Some were based on the erotic novelle of the Italians like *The Palace of Pleasure.* Others were less novels than pamphlets, and exposed the tricks practised by rogues on "rabbits". Greene wrote four booklets on this theme, "for the benefit of Gentlemen, Apprentices, Country Farmers and Yeomen". They became known as "Cony-Catching" pamphlets and detail very vividly the well-laid snares and traps set to catch bumpkins and other innocents unaccustomed to the wicked ways of London.

The Matter of Dragons

Yet with all this new reading-matter, the Elizabethans still dearly loved Pliny for he was full of marvels and wonders. "Dragons there are in Ethiopia", he says, "ten fathoms long" and few Elizabethans doubted or had any desire to doubt that this was so, although it is possible that some may have disbelieved that there were wild dogs with human hands and feet. And the exemplary conduct of the lion, though not a native beast, must certainly have reassured children. The king of the beasts was full of "nobleness and clemency and will sooner assail men than women and *never* young children unless it be for great famine".

The Elizabethan moppet sitting frog-eyed on his three-legged stool while an elder brother or sister read Pliny's *Natural History* aloud must have viewed the lion with an affection and composure unknown to the modern child whose monsters are men from Mars bent on destroying the earth. The sixteenth-century child must have delighted in the dolphin too, "the most swift fish of the sea" who above all other fishes loved "young children and the sound of instruments". The dolphin also loved the human voice and nothing rejoiced him more than to be addressed as "Simon".

Edward Topsell, one time chaplain of St. Botolph's, Aldgate, out-plinyed Pliny in the matter of dragons with his book *The History of Serpents*. From this, child and adult learned that the Ethiopian dragon was thirty yards long—a good ten yards longer than the measurements given by Pliny. One variety, the Epidaurian had a golden-yellow skin; another, a fierce mountain breed, was noted for its eyelids which rattled like brass. The Macedonian kind was the "most tameable" and fortunate Macedonian children kept these dragons as pets "riding upon them and pinching them as they would dogs without any harm and sleeping with them in their beds". . . .

The Elizabethans obviously must have divided dragons into two categories—good and bad. Henry Cowper the miller probably had a poor opinion of the dragon who damaged his mill. But those who had made the creature, meant him to represent the splendid golden dragon which long ago King Arthur's father had taken for his standard. It was this, the red-gold dragon of Wales, which the Tudor family bore as their badge and which, with the lion, now supported the English shield.

The dragon was one of Elizabeth Tudor's beasts.

Chronology

1533
Elizabeth, daughter of Henry VIII and Anne Boleyn, is born on September 7.

1534
The Act of Supremacy renounces obedience to the papacy; Henry VIII becomes head of the Church of England.

1536
Anne Boleyn, mother of Elizabeth, is privately executed on the Tower Green on a charge of treason.

1547
Henry VIII dies; Elizabeth's younger brother, Edward VI, becomes a figurehead king at the age of ten.

1549
The Book of Common Prayer is imposed; Catholic worship ends.

1553
Edward VI dies, Lady Jane Grey, cousin of Edward VI, assumes the crown on the basis of Edward VI's will; Mary Tudor, older sister of Edward VI and Elizabeth, raises an army and seizes the throne.

1554
Mary I imprisons Elizabeth in the Tower of London on the charge of treason; the queen releases Elizabeth when the charge cannot be proved.

1555
Mary I restores papal jurisdiction and Catholic worship in England.

1558

Elizabeth ascends the throne of England following the death of Mary I.

1559

Parliament enacts the Religious Acts of Settlement; England returns to Protestantism; Elizabeth I becomes head of the Church of England.

1562

John Hawkins and Francis Drake begin slave trade with the Spanish in the New World.

1563–1564

The plague breaks out in London, killing seventeen thousand people.

1568

Elizabeth's Catholic cousin, Mary, Queen of Scots, flees to England after being forced to abdicate the Scottish throne; soon after, rebellion arises aimed at installing Mary as ruler of England.

1569

Rebellion of the northern earls occurs.

1577

Sir Francis Drake embarks on a voyage around the world.

1583

Sir Humphrey Gilbert founds first English colony in America.

1585

War begins with Spain as England intervenes in support of a rebellion in the Netherlands against Spanish rule; Sir Walter Raleigh sends colonizing expedition to Roanoke, Virginia.

1587

Mary, Queen of Scots, is executed; Raleigh sponsors a second colonizing expedition to Roanoke.

1588

England defeats the Spanish Armada, marking the turning point between the era of Spanish world domination and the rise of Britain to the position of international supremacy.

1590

England temporarily halts attempts to colonize North America after Roanoke colony found abandoned; poet Edmund Spenser publishes *The Faerie Queene.*

1598

Elizabeth's closest adviser, William Cecil, Lord Burghley, dies.

1599

Globe Theatre opens with Shakespeare's *Henry V.*

1601

Robert Devereux, Earl of Essex, is executed for leading a revolt against Elizabeth's government; Elizabeth speaks to Parliament for last time.

1603

Elizabeth I dies on March 24 at Richmond Palace at the age of sixty-nine; James VI of Scotland is crowned James I of England.

For Further Research

Simon Adams, *Leicester and the Court: Essays on Elizabethan Politics.* Manchester, UK: Manchester University Press, 2002.

Stephen Alford, *The Early Elizabethan Polity.* Cambridge, UK: Cambridge University Press, 1998.

R.N. Ashley, *Elizabethan Popular Culture.* Bowling Green, OH: Bowling Green State University Popular Press, 1988.

Harold Bloom, ed., *Elizabethan Dramatists.* New York: Chelsea House, 1986.

Gamaliel Bradford, *Elizabethan Women.* Freeport, NY: Books for Libraries, 1936.

Arthur Bryant, *The Elizabethan Deliverance.* London: William Collins Sons, 1980.

Edward P. Cheney, *History of England.* Vol. 1. New York: Longmans, Green, 1926.

Anthony Esler, *The Aspiring Mind of the Elizabethan Younger Generation.* Durham, NC: Durham University Press, 1966.

Susan Frye, *Elizabeth I: The Competition for Representation.* New York: Oxford University Press, 1993.

Christopher Haigh, *Elizabeth I.* Essex, UK: Longman House, 1988.

E.E. Halliday, *Cultural History of England.* New York: Viking, 1967.

Richard Helgerson, *Forms of Nationhood: The Elizabethan Writing of England.* Chicago: University of Chicago Press, 1992.

Joanna Moody, ed., *The Private Life of an Elizabethan Lady: The Diary of Lady Margaret Hoby, 1599–1605.* Stroud, UK: Sutton, 1998.

Lena Cowen Orlin, *Elizabethan Households: An Anthology.* Washington, DC: Folger Shakespeare Library, 1995.

Roger Pringle, *A Portrait of Elizabeth I in the Words of the Queen and Her Contemporaries.* Totowa, NJ: Barnes & Noble Books, 1980.

R.E. Pritchard, ed., *Shakespeare's England: Life in Elizabethan and Jacobean Times.* London: Sutton, 1999.

Edmund Spenser, *The Faerie Queene.* Ed. Thomas P. Roche Jr. New Haven, CT: 1981.

Index